More from
THE TEXTILE ARTIST series

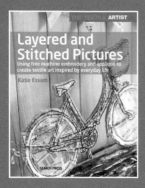

Layered and Stitched Pictures
978-1-78221-513-4

Layered Cloth
978-1-78221-334-5

From Art to Stitch
978-1-78221-030-6

Small Art Quilts
978-1-78221-450-2

Layer, Paint and Stitch
978-1-78221-074-0

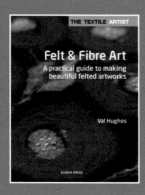

Felt & Fibre Art
978-1-84448-992-3

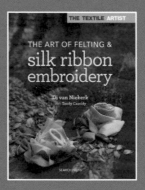

The Art of Felting & Silk Ribbon Embroidery
978-1-78221-442-7

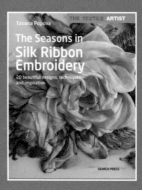

The Seasons in Silk Ribbon Embroidery
978-1-78221-655-1

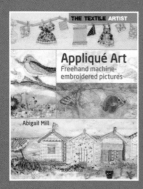

Appliqué Art
978-1-84448-868-1

EXPRESSIVE STITCHES

DEDICATION

Firstly I would like to dedicate my book to my husband,
Derek. His love, selflessness, patience and never-
ending support have allowed me to take over our lives
and create a book! It is hard to put into words his
encouragement and thoughtfulness. Thank you.
Grateful thanks to our three wonderful daughters,
Rebecca, Emma and Jessica, for their love and support,
for listening to all my self-doubts and for loving my work.
Annie, Tom, Lily and Beth – this is for you.
Finally, Mum, Joan Tomlinson who, like many other mums,
started my creative journey. She would be very proud.

Previous page
Abstract Meadow
91.5 x 91.5cm (36 x 36in)

*Linen base fabric. Vintage fabrics embellished onto the linen, followed by
different–coloured circles cut from plain fabrics. Hand stitches: straight
stitch, running/darning stitch. Turned edge, hem stitched to finish.*

This page
Venice Memory Cloth, No. 2
35.5 x 35.5cm (14 x 14in)

See page 105.

EXPRESSIVE STITCHES

A 'no rules' guide to creating original textile art

JAN DOWSON

SEARCH PRESS

ACKNOWLEDGEMENTS

Thank you Michelle Fuller and Graham Dawson for your support and guidance. Thank you Lynn Haith for your photography and support throughout – you have made some wonderful things happen.

A massive thank you to all my wonderful students over the years. You have mapped out my career, inspired me and finally given me the precious gift of 'A Pocket of Gold'. I will treasure it forever.

To Ruth Issett and Roz Dace who loved my work enough to make this book happen – thank you.

Thanks to the great team at Search Press, especially Emily Adam, my editor, who has been so supportive and encouraging. Thank you so much, Emily. Thank you also to photographer, Mark Davison, for his patience and brilliant photographs.

Thanks to Howard Bogod from Bernina for sponsoring me to use one of their wonderful machines, Bernina B476 Quilters Edition. It is a brilliant machine that has facilitated my work so well.

Thank you to Hilary Beattie and everyone at Art Van Go who send my orders so quickly and efficiently.

Thank you to Shirley Tierney for the loan of Mr. Crow, seen on pages 128 and 129.

So many people have played a part in my creative journey – my work colleagues, exhibition organizers and many more – who I haven't named as there isn't enough space! Thank you all so much.

Finally, I need to say a huge thank you to everyone who took part in nominating me for the prestigious awards I have received over the years; I have no words to describe how much it has all meant to me.

First published in 2021

Search Press Limited,
Wellwood, North Farm Road,
Tunbridge Wells, Kent TN2 3DR

Text, stitch diagrams and patterns copyright © Jan Dowson, 2021

Photographs on pages 17 and 18 by and are the copyright of the author.

Photographs on pages 6, 7, 9, 10, 11, 12br, 13, 14t, 14m, 15, 19, 20b, 21, 29b, 68 and 138–139 by Lynn Haith.

All remaining photographs by Mark Davison.

Photographs and design copyright © Search Press Ltd 2021

ISBN: 978-1-78221-750-3
ebook ISBN: 978-1-78126-706-6

The Publishers and author can accept no responsibility for any consequences arising from the information, advice or instructions given in this publication.

Suppliers

If you have difficulty in obtaining any of the materials and equipment mentioned in this book, then please visit the Search Press website for details of suppliers: www.searchpress.com

For more information about the author, her workshops and future exhibitions, please search for Jan Dowson - Textile Artist/Teacher on Facebook.

Contents

Above
Water Movement
43.25 x 51cm (17 x 20in)
*Hand couching covers the whole surface of the cloth, following
the undulating movement of water as the tide ebbs and flows.
A range of threads were used – thick, thin and fluffy fabric strips,
cottons and wools, some of which were hand dyed.*

Introduction

have always been creative in all aspects of my life. Everything to do with textiles and tactility – hand stitching, knitting, crochet and more – I have done since childhood. If anyone asked me if I came from a creative family, initially I might say no. However, after digging a little deeper for this book, I have realized the answer is actually yes – I did have lots of creative input, mostly as a child, and it has stayed with me.

Two very special elderly relatives had lots of influence on my creative journey. Preparing for an exhibition catalogue, I wrote:

'My work has formed from childhood memories: two elderly relatives – women who were not thought to be creative, but hardworking women living in a world of domestic discipline. Women with dreams of Bohemia encouraged me to see colour and 'feel' surfaces, giving me a new vocabulary, sowing the seeds and liberating the realization of ideas and feeling.'

One of these women was my Aunt Florence who ran a greengrocers. I remember her shop had no electricity, only gas mantels, right until the day it closed in the late Sixties. She was a great storyteller, but she also encouraged me to recognize and develop all my senses, and learn not only to appreciate colour but look – really look. There was a full set of Sylko thread drawers in the shop. I would sort and arrange each drawer of blues and purples, yellows and reds, blues and greens. As a child, looking into her wardrobe was my favourite thing – and you'd open the doors and the smell of moth balls would hit you! She would tell me stories about all her clothes – there were wonderful floral and patterned crepe dresses, fox fur collars, beautiful embroidered shawls – many of which had a fascinating life in the past, now never worn. She would describe colour and texture wonderfully, making connections to her favourite flowers and special moments in her life.

My Nana was very influential and, of course, Mum. Mum taught me to knit from an early age, along with basic sewing and embroidery skills – one of those embroidery stitches, lazy-daisy stitch, is still one of my favourite stitches today. We never had drawing paper in the house, so Mum would steam an envelope open until flat and then draw a grid at the centre, the squares about 2.5cm (1in) in size. I would have to fill each square with a pattern; she would then tell me to use my crayons and pencils to colour them in. It would keep me busy all day. I still have an obsession with the square: I carry a sketchbook or diary on me wherever I go, in which I develop patterns (they are more sophisticated these days!), and most of my work presents itself within a square or block.

My shelves of craft supplies, in my studio at home.

These creative beginnings taught me some valuable lessons that have stayed with me and play a strong part in my art today: to look whenever I can and wherever I am, and to feel – especially with colour, patterns and texture.

Once my daughters were in secondary school, I enrolled in the City & Guilds' (C&G) Creative Textiles qualifications, Part 1 and then Part 2. I then qualified in a Foundation in Art, along with some teaching qualifications. Over the next twenty years I taught C&G Creative Textiles L1 to L3 Diploma. I developed a huge collection of sketchbooks and creative stitch samples for my classes. Initially, I exhibited my own work, but then teaching and managing the creative art curriculum took over.

I loved teaching; it was my life, living and breathing textiles. My learners rewarded me by nominating me for a C&G Gold Medal of Excellence for Teaching, which I won. I was then selected for The Worshipful Broderer's Award; Princess Anne presented the award at Buckingham Palace. I then won The Beryl Dean National Teaching Award. During my last OFSTED inspection, when I was teaching C&G Creative Textiles and also managing the creative arts curriculum, an OFSTED inspector described me, and what was being achieved in my classes, as 'a pocket of gold in a field of dry grass'. I was bowled over; those words meant so much to me. I mentioned it to a friend and student,

Lynn, and she secretly decided to develop this phrase into a design for a retirement present from herself and my students. Students over many years were contacted and instructions were given to make a tag with a message for me and a pocket for it to sit in, following the theme of 'gold'. Lynn then made the book and box that would hold all the tags and pockets of gold. The precious gift was presented to me at our final end-of-year summer exhibition. It was a truly amazing undertaking, and the range and diversity of all the contributions was outstanding. It is the most beautiful and remarkable gift anyone could receive, and it still means so much to me.

Now that I am retired, I have been able to indulge in my own creative journey. I hope this book will allow you, the reader, to dive in and rediscover your own early memories, and hopefully start a creative journey of your own. Take some valuable time to sit down and think about your own inspirations. What are they? Where do they come from?

I hope the book will help you to record information, select appropriate stitches, develop interesting backgrounds, experiment with embellishments and maybe introduce you to working with three-dimensional pieces, too. Furthermore, I hope it will inspire you and enrich your creativity, and help bring together your ideas into a wonderful stitched cloth.

Working in my studio with my dog, Bertie, by my side.

Materials & tools

Embroiderers are spoilt for choice when selecting their resources, either for preliminary sketchbook work or for making their final designs. From fabrics and threads through to dyes and needles, there are so many products on the market that it can be quite daunting to know what to choose. For this reason, I hope my book will encourage you to take not only a simpler approach with the stitching process, but also with how you select your essential materials for your own work.

Collecting and searching for fabrics and threads is so enjoyable once you get started, but it is worth being mindful about the way they are stored, too. For me, it is part of the whole experience. I collect old baskets, tins and boxes, and it creates a lovely, meaningful relationship between the resources and the making process. My studio is a very much a 'nest-like' place, and I like to surround myself with all my treasures.

Fabrics

It is important for me to have integrity within the cloths I stitch. Integrity for me is an honesty in design, and giving real meaning to the stitched pieces I produce. Vintage fabrics fall into this group, as more often than not they are beautifully made and are of very good quality. They frequently form an important part of the development for many of my pieces, and it can mean that I have to look in unconventional places for my fabrics. Look at home first for inspiring old fabrics you could use in your work; you could even recycle clothes, or hot wash and shrink an old woollen garment.

Once you begin to look for fabrics in this way, you can start to see the textures of your fabric in a new light, and use this new knowledge to find amazing materials in places beyond your home, too: car-boot sales, jumble sales, charity/thrift/op shops and social-media sites are great places to scout for new materials. Have a look for items like:

- vintage cotton and silk
- vintage furnishing fabrics (I tend to use this mostly for broderie perse; see page 46 for details on this)
- linen
- sari silks
- old lace
- wool blankets
- old handkerchiefs.

Dyeing gives new life or interest to older fabrics, so do not write off a promising material if the colour is not quite right. Hand dyeing recycled fabrics will also help to blend and unify different types of fabric that you may need for a project. Vintage embroidery cloths in particular dye really well, as they tend to be made of natural fibres that are untreated. The embroidered areas also blend beautifully with the dye. Similarly, old damask tablecloths dye very well, with a lovely woven pattern and sheen that is still there after dyeing. If dyeing is something you have not done before, do not worry; I will show you the method I use on page 38.

Deliberately ageing and distressing fabric is also a great way to enhance newly bought fabrics. Simply dipping them in tea or coffee suddenly gives the fabrics a vintage look! Spotting the fabric with bleach using a brush or bleach pen is also good way to distress it.

As my cloths are intensely stitched, I like to choose fabrics that are lovely and soft to hold, hence my preference for the vintage fabrics listed. I do incorporate heavy furnishing fabrics and tightly woven fabrics in my pieces, but usually only in small amounts.

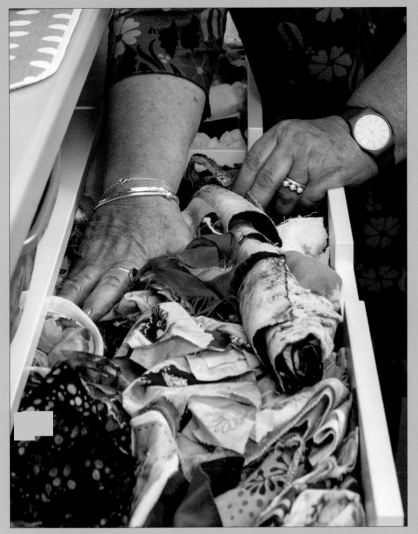

Threads

As with fabrics, look in unconventional places for your threads – car-boot sales, jumble sales or even spools inherited from elderly family members. Colours rarely matter, because they can simply be dyed to the shade you prefer. Whenever possible I like to use hand-dyed threads as they not only bring more cohesion to my work (since I tend to dye my fabrics at the same time), but also create a more personal, bespoke design.

I wind my hand-dyed threads onto old dolly/clothes pegs, vintage bobbins, old wooden cotton bobbins and twigs cut from trees in the garden. I then like to display these in my studio in old wooden boxes… Bliss.

On your search, have a look for threads such as:

- DMC coton à broder
- Knox's linen skeins
- white stranded cotton
- lace-making threads
- knitting cottons (stranded to make them easier to stitch with)
- silk threads.

I also use bought threads, and I particularly love to buy linen yarn. Of course, when I go to a show, I come back with lots of lovely threads already space-dyed… What a treat!

Personally, I prefer to use single-stranded or twisted thread. I like to get straight into my hand stitching as soon as possible, and not spend lots of time fiddling with strands!

Stitching tools

- **Needles** As embroiderers, the needle is the most important tool we have. It is vital to have the correct needle for the job, as it has a very important job to do. It needs a sharp point and a large eye. For embroidering I use **chenille needles** in sizes 26 and 22, and a super-large one in size 14.

  If I am turning a hem on a bound outer edge on one of my cloths, or seaming two fabrics together by hand, I like to use a small needle – a **quilting needle** is perfect for those jobs. For this type of sewing it is difficult to get a neat finish if the needle is too big. When attaching embellishments such as beads, shells and buttons, it is necessary to have a **beading needle**; this is a long, fine needle with a tiny eye. I also use a very large, long **upholstery needle** when making my bird sculptures.

- **Pins and pincushions** I like to use pins that have a glass ball head, as I find them easier to slide into the fabric and easier to remove. Of course, using a pincushion to store them and keep them safe is essential! Making a pincushion is a fun and simple project, and there are plenty of free patterns you can find online.

- **Scissors** Large dressmaking shears are essential for cutting out the fabrics for your work. In addition, a selection of small, sharp, pointed embroidery scissors are useful for trimming threads. When my scissors get old and blunt, I like to use them for paper cutting – and make sure I mark them as such!

- **Rotary cutter and cutting mat** Occasionally I use these to cut out my fabrics quickly, especially if the pieces need to be square or rectangular.

- **Sewing machine** To enable some of the creative stitches I use in my work, a sewing machine that has lots of stitches and can free-motion embroider is ideal. I use a Bernina Sewing Machine, B475 Quilters Edition. It's a lovely machine for free-motion embroidery, it has large spools, I can embroider words, and there are just enough extra stitches. It's also very easy to use.

- **Embellisher machine** This looks like a sewing machine, but instead of a sewing needle and foot there are barbed needles for felting! Essentially, this machine needle felts your work without the need to do it by hand – ideal for creating threadless textures on large pieces of work and for attaching layers of fabrics without using thread, too. I use a Baby Lock; it has six barbed needles and is a real workhorse. I use it mostly for securing appliqué on my base cloths.

Mixed media

The work I produce is design based, and thus incorporates lots of different types of textures and other art forms in order to create work in fabric that is meaningful to me. My sketchbook plays an important role in the design process, and I use it to develop ideas from inspirational starting points, which often directly translate from paper onto fabrics: if I stamp the paper in my sketchbook, I will stamp my fabric too!

Art materials include:

- a range of sketchbooks in a variety of shapes and sizes (handmade books are lovely to work in too)
- pencils and pens
- acrylic paint and gesso
- oil pastels, Markal® paint sticks and wax crayons
- brushes, rollers and sponges
- dyes – these include Koh-i-noor water-based dyes and Procion® dyes
- stamps to print the fabric – these include lino and lino cutters, and bought stamps, but I sometimes cut out stamps from potatoes too!
- cutting mats, craft knives and a paper-folding tool
- cartridge paper for making stencils, along with a collection of bought stencils
- gel printing plate (such as Gelli Arts™).

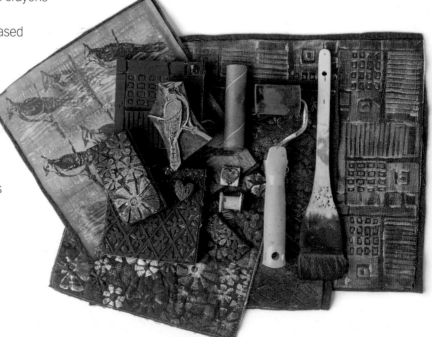

Inspiration

There is no limit to where inspiration can come from, and it can be from every aspect of our lives. It is so important that whatever you choose has a special meaning to you, and is not just something that happens to be on trend.

The best advice I can give you when getting started on a new project is to think about what is special to you; everything you observe can be a source of inspiration.

For example, do you have a favourite holiday destination or maybe a favourite walk – perhaps it is along a beach, or through a woodland? Think of items or colours associated with that location. Perhaps pattern or colour is your thing – do you like particular motifs on textiles or on artwork? Are you an animal lover? Animal prints, textures, birds, insects and beetles have lots of interesting shapes.

The landscape and its flora has always been an incredible source of inspiration – think about flowers and foliage, with their colours, patterning and form; or consider the weather, ever-changing and presenting myriad hues and shades you could represent in fabric; or maybe even the times of day, with the colours of the sun rising and setting. Architecture – historical or contemporary – and the details you can find in gates, stonework, metalwork or reflections in glass can be wonderful sources of textural inspiration.

Beyond physical examples, do explore your own emotional responses too, and look for ways to represent them. These can be memories, music, poetry, political issues or deep personal issues that have had a profound impact on you. I will go into a little more detail about this on the following pages.

It does not matter how or where you look – driving in the car, reading a magazine, listening to music – inspiration is there just waiting for you…

Places

Much of my own inspiration comes from several visits to Venice, Italy. It is my favourite place in the world, as it has amazing architecture that's filled with wonderful decorative detail. There is a richness of colour everywhere, accompanying this magnificent decorative detail, but I am also in love with the faded grandeur of the city – the decaying, peeling paint, the graffiti and slightly crumbling buildings – and it is the greys that stand out for me and which I choose to capture in my work, combined with complementary tints and tones (and a bit of glitz thrown in, to suggest Venice's glamorous past). I also cannot help but see this beautiful city in a grid – much like the squares I used to draw as a child! The shutters, windows, grilles and gates – squares jump out at me everywhere! So, it is a broken-up Venice, formed of dozens of intricate, patterned squares, that I choose to depict in my designs.

Closer to home, I also have (courtesy of my husband) the most beautiful natural garden, stuffed to the gunnels with trees and plants – a real urban oasis. I have produced a sketchbook from just the details I have spotted in and around the garden, sketched as little patterns within a grid design (I just cannot shake off grid pattern making; thanks Mum!). We have a lot of visiting birds, too: wrens, blue tits, blackbirds and seagulls that nest in our chimney pots, and a fabulously plump pair of wood pigeons that swing together harmoniously on a bird feeder. These birds are important in my life and work. A pleasure to watch, they are also full of character and texture. They are all perfect design inspirations.

Walks

Six years ago, I made the decision to retire. I now had more free time, and so as a present my husband bought me a much-wanted puppy, who we called Bertie. Having worked full time for so many years, having Bertie and taking him for a walk every day meant that, for the first time in years, I really saw and enjoyed the seasons around me.

We are very lucky to be surrounded by ancient woodland, and I regularly take lots of photographs as we walk, occasionally producing simple, quick sketches of a particular motif that inspires me. The hedgerows are magnificent in spring, accompanied by beautiful May blossom trees and my favourite plant, cow parsley. The Lincolnshire Wolds nearby are also very inspirational for landscape work.

I also live by the wonderful, natural coastline of north east Lincolnshire, UK, and we regularly have our walks along the beach. There is so much inspiration to be found by the coast, and it forms a wonderful, clean, linear view – strips of sea and sand, with textured sand patterns and tall grasses that grow along the paths.

The landscape immediately surrounding the beach is greatly inspirational, too. There are lovely meadow flowers that grow along the path in spring and summer; there is also a bird sanctuary that runs alongside the beach. I have made a real connection with some of the birds – I have my beautiful 'beach crows', whose feathers range from blacks to purples and greys, and who have strong legs, heavy beaks and sharp eyes. They have so much personality, sometimes walking by my side, playfully flying around me or landing on my head at times. They always seem happy to see me! There is also a pair of egrets I am fond of that I feed from the river inlet that flows into the sea...

Collections

I am an obsessive collector! There is so much you can find on your walks, and it can provide you with untold inspiration. On beach walks, I love to pick up driftwood, shells, bits of nets, lovely blue nylon cord, rusty metal and beach glass – in fact, I have yet to go on a beach walk that hasn't been productive in some way. I once found an amazing piece of striped heavy cotton that had torn away from a windbreak, blown in the wind, worn and weathered from tumbling in and out of the sea, which suddenly arrived at my feet.

It is always worth looking at the objects that catch your eye, and studying them with an artist's eye to see how they could be used in your work. For example, the shells I see on the beach near me have lovely barnacles growing on them, and look like little Victorian bonnets – they also seem to know I need them for embellishing, as they all have the perfect little hole for stitching them down! I have got a fabulous collection of sea glass, which I use to embellish cloth. Driftwood is also something I collect and use as perches or plaques for my birds.

I love to collect items from woodland walks, too. I often pick my favourite flowers – little white daisies in the grass, clover, leaves and cow parsley – then, In order to save them and capture their natural beauty, I press them and place them in my sketchbooks. I cannot resist picking up a few twigs too, covered in lichen; I have used them as weaving sticks, and even stitched them down into couched panels.

Recording

A sketchbook or visual diary is the best place to store source material; it is also, of course, the perfect place to record and develop new ideas.

Begin with those little treasures you collected on your walks, and use your sketchbook as a place to keep them all and inspire you. In fact, these stuck-in items have even ended up in the final design: I have laid found flowers between two sheets of polythene and then machine stitched around the outer edge of the page; this way, I can then pull the square out of the sketchbook and stitch the little patch into one of my memory cloths.

Use these items to help you remember your walks, and write down the thoughts they provoke. Take your sketchbook with you when you walk too, and explore feelings, immediate responses and spontaneous reactions you have when you are out there. Is it a windy day? Is it raining or snowing? What sounds can you hear? Bird song, people chattering and laughing, the noise of wind or rain – all of these sights and sounds encourage a personal, emotional response to your work. In fact, incorporating text in your actual work is a good way to literally convey and display feelings and emotions; often I hand- or machine-stitch poignant words or phrases, or stitch in existing labels that reflect my ideas. If you look at the work of Cornish painter Kurt Jackson, you can see how he includes words in his work, both in his sketchbooks and the finished paintings. Having such a literal depiction of the feelings you had when composing your design helps the viewer understand the artist's thoughts at the time of working, or provides a hint of the narrative.

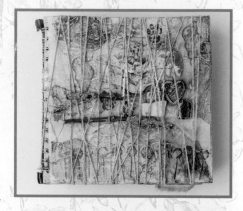

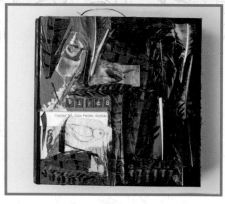

My sketchbooks

The outer covers of my sketchbooks are decorated to tell the story of the content, and in themselves act as an inspirational tool. The top book has been dip–dyed and wrapped with string, then twigs woven into the string, representing the theme of nature that runs throughout. With the bottom book, I have glued on feathers and images of birds to suggest this sketchbook's focus.

Ideas

Use your sketchbook as a place to play with mixed media and textures that inspired you at the very beginning of your journey. Here are some ideas about how you could use your sketchbook.

Make a collage – this really helps the development of ideas for your cloth, such as appliqué and the juxtaposition of surfaces.

Draw and develop favourite patterns – lift small areas of detail from an inspirational source to make a motif or repeat pattern.

Print – I like to make simple potato stamps and linocuts, and collect both new and vintage stamps (see page 42 for guidance on stamping).

Age and distress your sketchbook – use paints, dyes, bleach, tea or coffee to stain your pages; scrunching paper until it resembles fabric (see pages 22–25 for guidance on how you could do this).

Combine different media to make one piece of work – for example, develop a pattern or a simple detail in oil pastels and then wash over the work with ink or exhausted Procion® dyes. A drawing medium, such as a pen or pencil, can then be worked in the background to add more detail.

Here's another idea: a landscape piece can start with layers of torn paper that are glued into position on the page, then washed with ink followed by markings with a pen that is going to bleed when wet. Go in with another layer of markings, this time with a different pen that is fixed. Then maybe another wash of ink over all of this. When dry, pencil crayons can be worked in to give more detail. A design could also begin by printing the surface with acrylic paint. When the paints have dried, wash over with dyes, then work into the surface with metallic crayons. Add some fine pen marks. Building layers of mixed media this way helps with making decisions when layering fabrics for a finished piece. The marks that I make help me to decide where to place stitches.

Remember, your sketchbook is your private personal space, so do not be afraid to explore any ideas you have. Try new techniques, experiment and play! A free mind encourages a more creative, thoughtful work.

Creating a unique sketchbook

The importance of making a personal sketchbook is huge, in my opinion. Not everyone agrees, mind you; it is always a debatable topic.

Why do I keep a sketchbook? For me, a sketchbook is:

- a place to store thoughts and findings
- a place to work through and record ideas from your inspirational starting point
- a way of creating discipline in your working practice
- a place to self-evaluate and reflect
- somewhere to store the planning process that formulates the final work
- a visual space to record the development of finished work.

The sketchbook is such a valuable resource that can be used time and time again. It should be bursting with creative ideas. When starting a new body of work the sketchbook is always my first 'job', I then flit in and out of it as I develop stitched samples to try out my ideas. Once I am happy with these, I finally produce a final work.

It is important to remember that when selecting your inspirational starting point, it is only a starting point. The creative journey you take in your sketchbook will possibly change your initial thoughts and ideas. There is nothing wrong with this; the final design will be your idea's 'true' form, and become a unique work that has integrity at its heart.

Below are a few ways I like to personalize my sketchbooks before adding my ideas to them. By making the pages into colourful, textural spaces, the urge to create and fill the books with ideas and sketches is even greater.

Tear it up

Before I start, I like to customize a sketchbook by tearing the pages and changing the whole concept of the book. For example, fold and tear the first page in half lengthways; on page 2, fold and tear away half the page horizontally; page 3, tear a hole in the middle; page 4, fold and tear away only a quarter of the page; on page 5, cut a narrow rectangle out the page. Continue through the whole book in this way until each page has been cut away in some fashion. This will allow a glimpse of the next page to show through as you look through the book; it also takes away that scary brand-new book feeling!

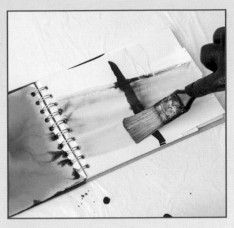

Colour your book

Take away the white space literally by painting all the pages in your sketchbook! Ensure that you have lots of different colours and brushes to hand, and that the surface you are working on is protected with a wipeable cloth. In addition, make sure there is a suitable place to leave your book to dry.

1 Prepare your coloured medium in as many colours as required in small jars I am using acrylic paint here, but you could use gouache, watercolour or even oil.

2 Using large paintbrushes, such as decorator's brushes, begin to paint colours onto each page, changing the colours as you go. Make sure you cover each page.

3 Colours will bleed together as you progress through the book.

4 When complete, lift the book, allow it to drip for a minute or two and stand it on your plastic table cover. As it stands open, gently open as many pages as you can and leave to start the drying process.

5 Each day, separate more pages until the whole book is now open.

6 It will take about a week to dry, depending on temperature and humidity.

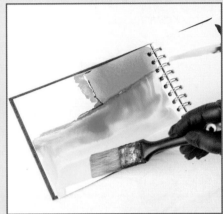

Dye your book

Dyeing your sketchbook is a wonderful way to add colour and interest to your pages, and the textures and effects left behind can be inspirational in themselves. With this method, it is not necessary to cut and tear pages as the book will disintegrate a little anyway.

You will need a tray big enough to lay your sketchbook in (a cat-litter tray is perfect); dyes, such as exhausted Procion® dyes or inks; a wipeable cloth to protect your surface; and a suitable place to leave your book to dry.

This method of customizing a sketchbook will make it a bit more difficult to draw on the pages – or will it dictate a different drawing medium?

1 This time we are going to mix up colour in your tray. It can be a mix of colours or a walnut ink that will give you a lovely aged look.

2 Lay your sketchbook in the tray of liquid. Swish it around a bit so the front and back cover soak up the colour.

3 Start to open the book, a page at a time, making sure each page is well soaked in colour.

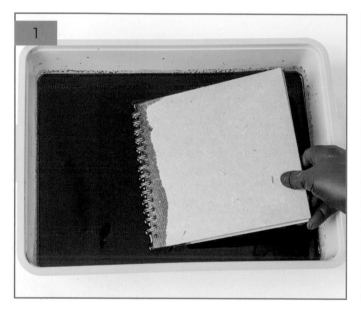

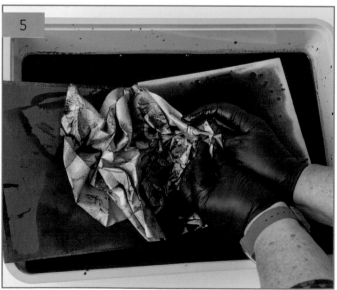

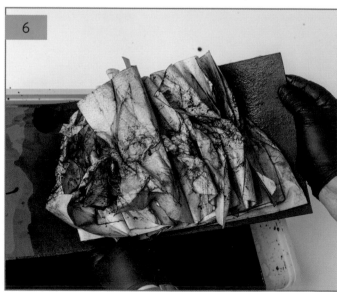

4 Carefully turn back to the first page of the sketchbook and very gently scrunch the page as much as you dare. You do not want the page to tear away from the book.

5 Move on to the next page and scrunch it as before.

6 Work your way through the book, scrunching each individual page until you have reached the last one. You will now have an open book with a huge pile of scrunched paper!

7 Lift the sketchbook out of the tray, tilt it and give it a little shake to release any excess dye, then place it on the plastic cloth. The book will take a week or two to dry.

8 When it is almost dry, take it to your ironing board and iron each page flat. This may cause a bit of decay: some pages will have holes or corners missing. Some pages may have stuck together which will entail a bit of distress when separating – this is no problem, and is all part of the ageing process. The result should be wonderful creased pages that have taken the dye into the creases, beautifully ageing them.

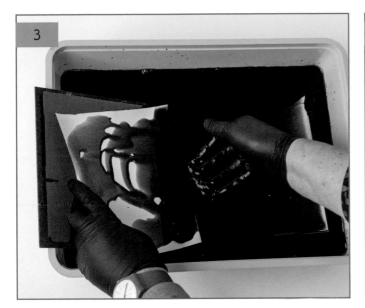

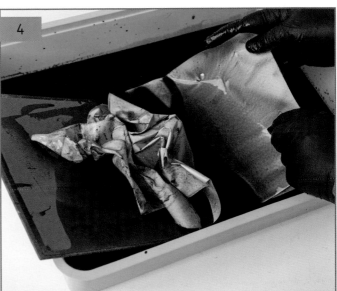

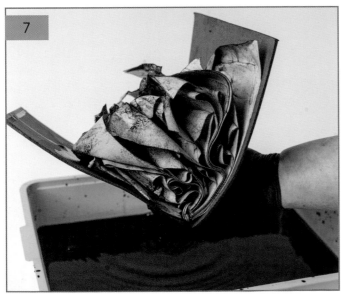

Playing with colour

Once the inspirational starting point has been chosen, collect as much visual material as you can from magazine pictures and photographs you have taken, to develop your own drawings and sketches. Social-network websites dedicated to imagery, such as Pinterest and Unsplash, have good quality photographs to explore and inspire. Remember to use these images as sources of inspiration only, and not something to imitate. There is a greater pleasure in creating something yourself, than in copying another's work.

There are lots of ways to get started with your development – abstraction, pattern development, simplifying, identifying detail, etc. – but for me the most important start is to identify my colour palette. Colour is one of the most fundamental design elements. All the work you develop in your sketchbook relies on your colour scheme. It will likely change as you continue to establish your final design, as some colours will become more dominant in your final piece than others, but to get your colours identified at the beginning will reap rewards. It is important that you look – really look – at the colours within your inspirational starting point. How many colours are there? You will be amazed at the choices you make and the colours that will (or won't!) work, once you start your investigation.

Making a colour grid

If you are an organized person, you may like to draw out a separate grid of 2.5cm (1in) squares, with at least 10 squares to a grid. It's good to use a range of colour media – crayons, acrylic paint, Koh-i-noor, Procion® dyes, pastels and more – and then mix them all up, or just use a single favourite colouring medium. Colour each square in your grid with the different colours you see in your source material; you may need to mix colours together in order to get the full range of colours you need.

A much simpler approach, and the one I usually use, is to paint a little square or rectangle of paint directly onto the page, or get creative and fill a page with splodges, splatters, blocks, lines and dribbles.

The whole process could take as little as 30 minutes. It's not about creating a work of art but creating a valuable resource, a set of colours that are guaranteed to work well together and that will also help you work out the colour palette for your next design. At the end of the day, you will have produced a colour palette that can be referenced throughout the project.

Study your subject for colour inspiration

Find as many colours as you can within your inspirational starting point. From this, there will be a set of colours that jump out at you. Don't panic if you see lots of colours in your subject – choose just a few that really strike you at first observation, and then use these for your work. It would be overwhelming to use too many colours in your palette. In any case – 'less is more', as they say.

Pressed flowers

I love to collect wild flowers when out walking. When I return home I press them, and they form part of my sketchbook development. The page above depicts butterweed, a yellow daisy–like weed. When dried, the colour becomes dulled, more mustard than yellow. This particular sketchbook was exploring tonal values, using layers of mustard yellow and greys. It will eventually inform the narrative of a landscape panel, or the whole cloth.

Mark making

Mark making is a term used to describe the lines, textures and rendering techniques that artists use when developing a drawing or a design. It enables us to be more expressive with our development. Marks are everywhere we look – lichen on a garden wall, graffiti, pen doodles, freckles on a face, hair lines, scratches and gouges on paintwork and metal surfaces. As soon as we have drawn a simple line or signed our names on a piece of paper, we have made a mark.

I like to use a range of pens and pencils to create texture and marks – crosshatching, arrangement of lines, tiny little circles, dots and scribbles. Ultimately, these will suggest the stitches I will use in the final design. For a more expressive mark, I like to use oil pastels, and then run a wash over the pastels using ink. Water-soluble pencils and pens are also great for the expressive marks.

Mark making is an excellent technique for separating layers and spaces in a landscape, and is a valuable technique for any design development work. Marks are essential to drawing; we start with a blank piece of paper and rely on simple marks or lines that are made with drawing media to begin the drawing process. The marks don't stand alone but rely on the media used and the surface they are drawn on.

Experimenting with different media

Producing a wide range of mark-making techniques with a variety of media will help to inform your ideas for stitches later. Look at the samples right and select a few examples...

- No. 1 dashes – seed stitch
- No. 1 circles – detached chain stitch
- No. 1 triangles – fly stitch

With any chosen mark that is going to be replicated into stitch, try to use a range of thread thicknesses. Heavy texture can be gained by piling up stitches or wrapping stitches with another thread – I will go into detail about this in the chapter 'Expressive hand stitches' (see page 52).

Stars	Triangles	Dashes	Circles
1	1	1	1
2	3	4	5
6	7	3	6
7	6	2	4

1 rOtring 0.5mm fineline

2 Layers of oil pastel, scratched

3 Soft pastels, blended

4 LYRA Aquacolor

5 Oil pastels, blended

6 Oil pastel marks, washed with ink

7 Pencil crayons

Planning the marks in a landscape cloth

This page in my landscape sketchbook demonstrates a range of mark making techniques. The paper of the page has been torn into horizontal layers before I started the work (see also page 22). After this, the marks have been developed using a range of media including a Pigma Micron 005 pen. This helps me to define layers and contours of the landscape, as well as colour and possible stitch marks – valuable when developing the finished cloth.

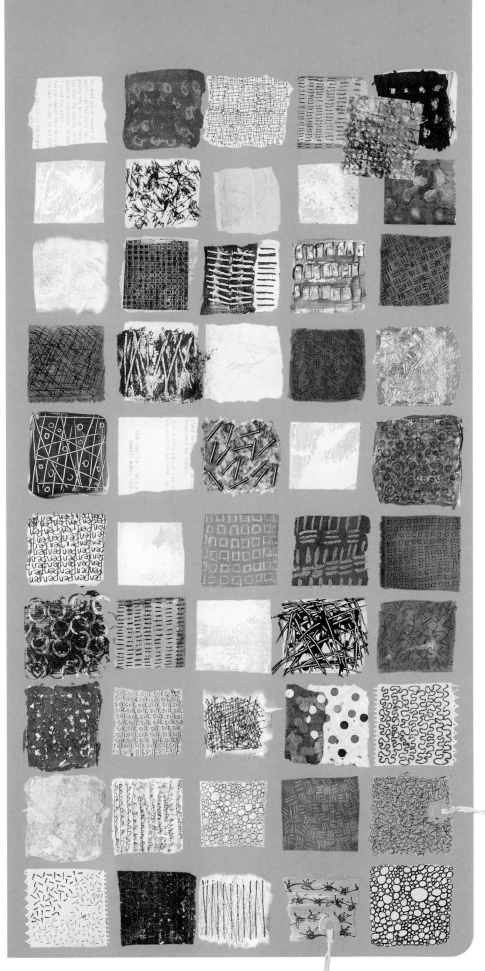

Making a marking grid – 'The 50 square challenge'

This exercise will challenge your skills and encourage you to play with a wide range of techniques and media. Use these 7.5cm (3in) square mark-making studies to help you choose your favourite pattern and rendering, which you can then translate into a selected range of stitches for your final work. Enjoy!

1 In your sketchbook draw out 10 rows of five 7.5cm (3in) squares, so that there are 50 squares on your paper.

2 Work each square randomly to create a range of surfaces. For example, you could glue down newsprint, calico, brown paper or tissue paper, or simply paint the square with gesso.

3 When all squares are ready, select a range of mark-marking media – graded pencils, graphite sticks, Conté crayons, Aquarelle pencils, pens, dip pens and ink, felt-tip/marker pens, wax crayons or oil pastels, and ink and charcoal pencils.

4 Produce different tonal rendering marks within each square – lines, cross-hatching, dots, tiny circles and more – to highlight each media used and its full tonal effects.

5 Explore and experiment with marks that can be created in a physical way, too: hole punching, stapling, cutting with a scalpel, folding, printing, making rubbings, hand stitching, gluing on layers of torn paper and adding scrunched tissues.

From mark to stitch

Landscape sketchbooks

A selection of landscapes that have been developed from initial quick sketches. You can see that all the pages in my landscape sketchbook have been torn before starting the work. The torn lines become an integral part of the development. The emphasis is then to define each layer of the landscape with mark making, colour and texture.

Top: On the left-hand side of the sketchbook, torn holes in the page allow a glimpse of the previous page. A little wash of ink was applied to the background before mark making. A range of pens and pencils were used including an Edding 55 Fineliner pen, which blends with water, and a white Conté crayon for the highlights. The perspective is developed by using small dots and circles for the distant fields, and drawing large, bold marks in the foreground – these include grasses and cow parsley. Layers and layers of marks built up this depiction of the location, the Lincolnshire Wolds, UK.

Middle: On these pages there are lots of textures, and staples are also used as marks. Some of the papers that were torn from the book have been glued back on the page, which helps to build an interesting surface.

Bottom: Again, lovely torn pages. I have used large stitches to reconnect the torn pages on the left-hand side of the sketchbook. Using a range of marks, such as cross-hatching, circles and scribbles, gives the impression of the various layers and elements that make up a landscape – invaluable when designing the final landscape. in stitch.

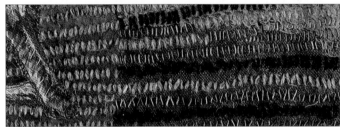

Mark making in the final stitched landscapes

The final landscape cloths are not worked from my landscape sketchbook directly, but are loose interpretations that acknowledge the inspirational source, colour and form. However, there is a very strong link to the mark making in the sketchbook and the final stitches. The time spent in my sketchbook informs me of the appropriate stitches to create marks that separate areas and layers within the landscape of the cloth.

Top three details
Close ups of *Two Hares in a Landscape*
Full work on page 84.

Top left: Lazy-daisy stitches sit behind the hare – a lovely, textured stitch.

Top right: Straight stitches in groups of three are worked in different directions to create cross-hatching marks.

Middle right: Rows of straight stitch in different weights of thread.

Right detail
Close up of *Meadow Landscape with Two Hares*
Full work on page 87.

A block of detached chain stitch [A], little straight stitches that form lovely star-like marks for the distant meadow area [B], cross-hatching [C] and rows of running stitch [D].

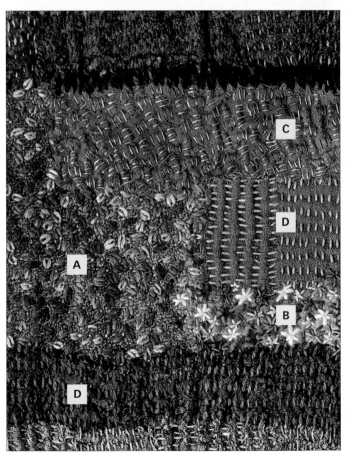

Developing expressive work

All of the elements I explore in my sketchbooks play an important part in the creation of my final work. I have many sketchbooks, and each one is dedicated to a particular composition or theme that I am unconsciously putting together in my mind, added fragmentally to the pages of my book over time. A design I have been brewing then comes to fruition when I reach a stage where I 'feel' I have everything I need; I then pull all these abstract, thematic elements together to create a cohesive work that reflects the story I've been wishing to tell in fabric and stitch. So, before we delve into my key techniques, let's see how you can take all your sketches and collections to prepare a design.

Making a plan

Working from rough sketches and preliminary sketchbook drawings, I plan out the composition on a large sheet of paper. This is usually a very simple linear design, with small suggestions of where additional motifs or embellishments will go.

Next I make a 'cartoon', a rough design to scale, before starting the fabric piece. The rough draft is not a fine-art drawing, but a very quick sketch of the basic outline of the composition. For me, this is an important process, as it allows me to get a sense of the overall size of the work. At this stage, I may need to make adjustments to the design in order for it to work at a large scale.

In order to achieve the final desired size, often I tape sketchbook pages together to make a larger piece of paper. For large commissioned pieces that have been approximately 2.25 x 1.25m (7 x 4ft), I have used lengths of lining wallpaper that are then taped together!

Once I have the full-sized sketch I can then decide if it needs more work to get the perspective right. I may also splodge some colour on, usually Procion® dye, as this helps me to work out the different perspectives in the piece.

This process works very well with landscape pieces. I have also used this technique when developing large decorative panels where there may be a repeat pattern involved, which has to be worked to actual scale.

Preparing your fabric

We've covered briefly the sort of fabrics and thread to look out for prior to starting a design (see page 8) and I'll explain later how you can add further interest and texture to your fabrics and threads through dyeing (see pages 38–41). While each of my key designs vary slightly at this preparation stage, I do follow a similar process to set up the base of my design: it is worth remembering that your plan is not written in stone; as the piece develops, your creativity will allow you to add or take away. For example, you may have decided in your development work that you are not going to add any embellishments – but then you suddenly have the urge to add buttons, beads or decorative stitches! This isn't wrong; it's good to make spontaneous changes, and to let yourself go with the flow.

Select a base fabric that is a little bit bigger than your final intended size. This can be any fabric, but make sure it is not too heavy or too tight, because it is going to have a range of fabrics layered onto it, and it still needs to be soft and pliable for stitching. I like to use recycled linen for this. The colour doesn't really matter, as the whole surface will be completely covered.

Select the fabrics that will make up the main surface of your composition. These will sit on top of your base fabric. Use your plan to help you with this, choosing them based on the colours and textures that reflect those you captured in your sketchbook. Remember, these will be either dyed, printed on or embellished – or all of these! – so you may need to visualize how the final fabrics will sit on your base.

It may take some time to arrange the composition. Keep moving fabrics around, trying different colour combinations. You can happily continue to play with your fabrics until you are satisfied that you have achieved a cohesive, balanced arrangement of colour and texture.

When you are happy with your 'layers', they can be tacked/basted together. Avoid using bonding agents to anchor down your fabrics onto the base fabric. These tend to stiffen the fabrics a little and, remember, we are aiming for a lovely soft cloth to stitch: the needle needs to softly glide through the fabrics, enabling a satisfying and relaxing stitching process. Once the tacking/basting is complete you can work over with the embellisher. This will stop any movement in the small patches of cloth completely.

Arranging your composition

It's worth spending some time assembling your composition, especially if it involves several layers of fabric. Once you are happy, the layers can then be tacked/basted then embellished together. (See page 44 for more information on embellishing, and page 88 for this project.)

35

Expressive techniques

As you will now have learnt, sketchbook development helps you to understand how to convey your ideas and feelings in order to create work that is expressive and has integrity – be they emotive, powerful, meaningful or whatever you wish. Producing expressive work is about trying to encapsulate those feelings through equally expressive techniques. There are many ways of doing this. This may be hand-dyeing your own fabric and thread to create the right mood. I love to use a range of appliqué techniques to give my work meaning, then either use the embellisher machine to soften the surface, apply shape, and perhaps soften the colour and push back detail if required, or apply free-motion embroidery stitches to deliberately turn those shapes into defined forms and create marks.

Hand embroidery, and using hand stitches expressively, is the most important part of my work. The stitched surface can create powerful texture or add gentle rhythms to the piece.

Found objects – sea glass, beach ceramics, feathers, tiny pebbles or lichen-covered twigs – that are used to embellish and decorate the surface of a cloth are secured by glue or stitches to create a richness across the surface of your work like no other.

The following pages will describe the various techniques I use to create my main body of work. Not all of these processes are combined to create a single piece of work – sometimes I may only select three or four, depending on the design – but they are arranged in the order I recommend when embarking on your own piece of work. I hope this section of the book will inspire your own processes, and perhaps encourage you to try a new technique and bring some emotional responses to your work.

Dyeing fabric & threads

Dyeing my own fabrics and threads has been part of my work from the very beginning. I like to work with a large range of fabrics, some of which are vintage cloths that have been previously embroidered or damask tablecloths that have a gorgeous design woven into them. Hand dyeing brings out the pattern of the fabric even more, and creates a cohesive colour palette throughout all my fabrics and threads.

When I am having a dyeing session, I tend to throw everything into my vintage enamel mixing bowls – these are large bowls that will hold quite a lot of fabric and thread, from bits of old lace, cotton tape and cotton buttons, to cottons, linen, silks, recycled shirts and patchwork-patterned fabrics. They all take the dye differently, and yet work so well together. There is nothing more satisfying to me than ironing a new batch of newly dyed fabrics – ironing out the wrinkles is when you can really see the colour blends exposed… Magic!

I like to spoon dye directly onto the fabric, rather than soaking the latter in a dye bath. I also prefer to use cold-water dyes; these are fibre reactive, meaning they fix to the fabric chemically, rather than being forced with heat like many common dyes. For this reason, cold-water dyes are often used to dye naturally-made fabrics that have come from plant material, such as cotton, linen, silk, rayon and viscose. (Viscose and rayon fabric are made from cellulose – a substance made from bamboo, plant and tree pulp.) The lovely vintage fabrics I collect are therefore perfect for the job, as these are almost always made of natural fibres. Likewise, my threads are typically made of cotton, linen and silk, all of which are natural fibres and nice to dye. If cold-water dye is used on a synthetic fabric, the dye will just run off as they have no natural protein to fix to chemically.

My preferred brand of cold-water dye is Procion®. The dyes are easy to mix and give a good vibrant colour to the fibres. Once the dye has lost its chemical strength, I use its 'exhausted' version as ink for papers and initial sketchbook work. As the ink still dyes fabric, but does not fix so well, it is also perfect for creating samples of designs prior to making the final piece. Nothing is wasted.

There is a wide range of colours available for dyeing. My own set consists of only six colours – lemon yellow, turquoise, pearl grey, magenta, rose brown and warm black – but in different combinations and mixed together, they give me a wider colour palette.

HEALTH & SAFETY

- Procion® dye in its initial state is a very fine, chemical powder, so a good face mask must be worn to avoid ingestion. Once the dye has been mixed with a little hot water, which dissolves it, the mask can be removed.
- When mixing dye, always wear protective clothing such as a protective garment, rubber gloves, goggles and a mask.

- Any equipment used for dyeing must be solely dedicated to fabric dyeing. **Do not reuse containers or spoons for food preparation**.
- Use soap and water to remove any dye that comes in contact with the skin. **Do not use bleach**. For stubborn dye stains use a specialist skin cleaner, such as Reduran.

Cold–water dye recipes

With cold-water dyes, an acid and alkaline solution needs to be made first that is then added to the dye, in order to help fix the dye to the fabric. Once mixed, I label the bottles for each solution and store them away from light.

Acid – salt or urea solution drives the dye into the fibres.

Alkaline – soda water or soda ash solutions react with both the fabric and the dye to bond and fix the dye.

Acid   *Alkaline*

Basic acid & alkaline solution recipes

Alkaline

Make a soda-water solution – 200g (7oz) washing soda mixed with 1L (35floz) of very hot water
OR
make a soda-ash solution – 20g (5 tsps) soda ash mixed with 1L (35 floz) of very hot water.

Acid

Make a salt-water solution – 750g (26½oz) of salt mixed with 1L (35 floz) of very hot water
OR
make a urea solution – 140g (5oz) of urea mixed with 1L (35 floz) of warm water.

Main dye recipe

1 Mix 1 teaspoon of dye with a tablespoon of hot water.

2 Add 25ml (5 teaspoons) of soda-water or soda-ash solution and 25ml (5 teaspoons) of salt or urea solution to the mix.

3 Top up the mix with cold water, about 300–425ml (10–14 floz). The more water, the weaker the colour.

What to do:

1 Assemble your pieces to dye. Once you have decided on your colour scheme, make up pots of dye using the recipes on page 39.

2 In a bowl of soda-ash solution, wet your chosen fabrics or threads thoroughly, rubbing out any sizing agents or finish with gloved hands. Once you're satisfied you've removed as much as you can, leave them to soak in the solution for an hour or so – the fabric or threads need to be wet enough so that the dyes flow through the fibres evenly.

3 Arrange enough small containers or food bags for each colour combination you want to make.

4 For variegated shades, spoon the dyes over your fabrics or threads. Make sure you push the dye into the fabrics or threads with the spoon. Leave for a minimum of 25 minutes. This is a good time to clean up any messy areas! If time allows, fabrics and threads can be left in the dye for several hours before rinsing; the colour may be a little stronger, that's all. Don't worry if you have to go out; no harm will come to the fabric.

5 When ready, rinse the fabrics or threads in cold water until the colour runs clear.

6 Leave the items to dry completely. You will need to iron dyed fabrics before using them for your designs.

Dyed designs

Right: A range of vintage fabrics in white and cream were layered onto a ground cloth. Decorative hand embroidery was then worked along each band of fabric using neutral-colour threads. Once the cloth was completed and all the embroidery done, Procion® dyes where painted directly onto the stitched fabric and I allowed the colours to bleed from one layer to the next. The dye was left to set and then the cloth rinsed in the usual way.

Below, top: Using a hand-made linocut, the fabric was printed using acrylic paint (see pages 42 and 43). Once the paint was dry, Procion® dyes were painted over the surface. Finally, lazy-daisy stitches were embroidered into each diamond, the thread itself dyed to echo the rainbow effect of the fabric underneath.

Below, bottom: Hand-dyed calico was cut into tiny narrow strips of varying widths. Each strip was randomly selected and couched together onto a base fabric.

TIP

You don't need to use white fabric or threads as a base for dyeing – pale and pastel colours work well too. The important thing for a successful cold-water dye is that the materials you choose are made from natural materials, else they will not take the dye.

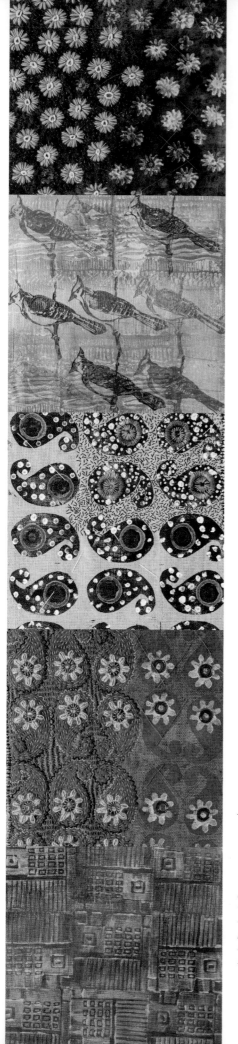

Printing, stamping & stencilling

Printing is a simple process that can produce a beautiful and complex surface pattern. One of the very earliest art forms, printing has been a means of decorating surfaces all around the world, and over many thousands of years. It is also an excellent technique for developing your sketchbook work. In the sketchbook dedicated to my recordings of my trip to Venice, I have produced several linocuts inspired by the grid patterns and architectural details I saw there.

Where do I print? Mostly in my sketchbooks, as part of the initial recording and development process. Over the years I have bought a fabulous collection of stamps and stencils that work with my design sources, either replicating the patterns in the source that catch my eye the most, or reflecting their theme.

As a great deal of my printing is inspired by design sources, most of my stamps and stencils are made by hand. Hand-made stamps can include linocuts, India rubbers cut into with a scalpel to create tiny patterns, or a make-up sponge. If a quick stamp is needed to develop an impromptu pattern, I might even carve a potato for printing – there is always a potato in the vegetable bin!

If I want a quick stencil, I simply use cartridge paper. Sometimes, I already have a pattern prepared in my sketchbook, and this can be transferred to paper to make a stencil. To transfer the stencil design from my sketchbook, I either trace it off or make a rubbing if the pattern has a textured surface. Once it has been decided which bits of the design need to be cut away, I use a craft knife and a cutting mat to cut out sections of the paper; I then paint both sides of the paper with PVA glue so that my hand-made stencil can be used time after time.

Printing also produces wonderful and intricate textiles. Combined with stencilling, printed fabric provides a rich, vibrant and exciting surface pattern that is perfect for stitching – either with hand stitches or with free-motion embroidery on a sewing machine – as the details of the pattern can be enhanced and outlined. For my memory cloths and birds, I will often print the whole of the fabric used; in my stitched landscapes, printing is done in small areas of detail, to add flowers, trees or text, for example.

Once the printing, stamping or stencilling – or all three – is complete on paper or fabric and the machine work done, some hand stitching can be added to give extra detail in a particular area.

From print to stitch

All the fabrics left have been printed with acrylic paint. When the paint is dry, exhausted Procion® dye is painted over the printing to colour the background fabric. The bottom three designs were printed with handmade stamps; for the top two I used bought stamps. Stitching enriches and enhances the printed pattern further. Stitch choices come to me quite spontaneously; however, you could print the pattern onto paper and use this to develop a stitch plan, drawing marks to suggest where to place them and which will work with your pattern. Select different stitches for each element of the pattern, and perhaps play with complementary coloured threads – this will bring areas of the design to prominence and push some areas back.

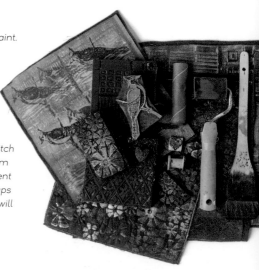

What to do:

Here are a few key things to know about printing, stamping and stencilling before you begin:

- To print, you need a soft surface to work on – this is vital for printing, so that you can get into the crevices of the surface.
- Acrylic paint works perfectly on fabric as well as paper – once it's on, it stays on! Emulsion tester pot paints are good for printing, too.
- Complementary colours are ideal, so that one print knocks back the strength of the next.
- I prefer to work on a plain base, rather than one with an existing pattern, as it allows the design I'm creating to come into its own. This applies to both fabric and paper.
- The choice of stamps and stencils in your sketchbook will inform the development of the final piece.

TIP

Transfoil gives a fabric surface a gilded effect. Cut or tear little pieces of fusible webbing (just the soft glue from the back of the paper) and place them onto your design where you would like the highlights/metallic effects. Protect the area with non-stick baking parchment, and with a hot iron, iron the webbing in place on the fabric. Remove the baking parchment. Place a sheet of Transfoil over the webbing sections, colour side up, and then use the outer edge of a cool iron to rub in the Transfoil. Let it cool for a couple of seconds then gently pull away the Transfoil. You will be left with a beautiful gilded area on your cloth where the foil has glued to the fabric. Repeat as many times as you need to get the desired effect you want.

In the sample below, I wanted to give the circular filling stitches more shine. I tore off small pieces of fusible webbing, placed them over my chosen areas with the glue side down, then used a hot iron to adhere them to the fabric. I left the webbing pieces to cool for a moment then peeled away the backing papers. I then had areas of glue on my fabric, ready for silver Transfoil.

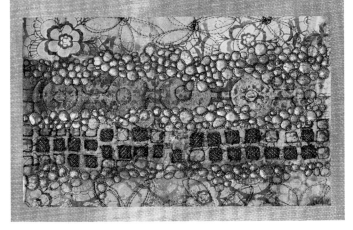

1 Print first to develop an initial pattern.

2 Add the stencil and stamping designs to create foreground design.

3 Finish with a wash of exhausted Procion® dye, ink, watered-down fabric paint or watered-down acrylic paint, to make the whole design more cohesive.

Using an embellisher

After your fabric is chosen, and perhaps dyed and/or printed, your fabrics can be arranged over your base fabric to create the beginnings of your composition. The arrangement can be simply tacked/basted together, but in some cases the layers can be embellished together – ideal if there are lots of little, fiddly pieces of fabric in the design.

To embellish, you will need a machine aptly called an embellisher. Originally designed for the purpose of appliqué (and you'll see why in a moment), the embellisher is also known as a felting machine because it works like a mechanized needle-felting needle – the fibres of the top fabric are pulled through the layers to the base fabric, hooking them together.

There are multiple reasons why I use an embellisher, but primarily I use it to secure several appliqué pieces and fabric layers together as it not only allows me to create a multi-fabric background in a single, quick process, it also creates a varied, textured fabric background that's flat enough for the details I add later. Details, such as hand stitching, would be very difficult to execute on a very layered, loose background. The result embellishing creates is a soft, pliable fabric with a seamless patchwork of colour and pattern. The embellisher also creates a lovely ripple effect across the surface, too.

For those of you who may not have an embellisher, or have not had chance to use one, the process is so simple. The machine itself looks just like a sewing machine, and is used very similarly – there is a foot pedal, a top tension and you can move the fabric around as you would for free-motion machine embroidery. However, there are some significant differences: the machine has no bobbin or thread, and comes with a set of barbed needles, placed in the machine as a ring of needles that punch down into the fabric all at once for a speedy result.

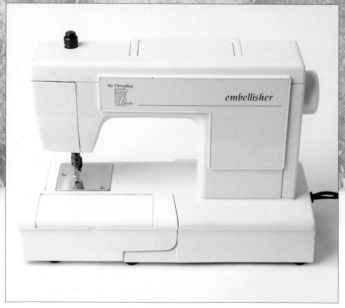

Embellisher

My Baby Lock embellisher, which I've had for years.

Embellisher needles

Depending on the model of embellisher (and your own needs), there can be five to 12 needles in the machine; mine has six. It has a see-through finger guard around the needles, allowing you to see where you're working but also preventing your fingers from getting too close to the needles.

What to do:

If I am working with lots of tiny fabric pieces, initially I tack/baste the fabrics to the base fabric with large running stitches and a hand needle, just to make sure I don't lose any of them while I am getting the work under the embellisher. Larger fabric pieces are added as I work.

To use the embellisher, simply put your foot on the pedal, just like a sewing machine, and move the fabric around under the needles to secure the layers. As they enter the layers of fabric, the barbed needles punch down tiny bits of thread from the top fabric and pull up tiny bits of thread from the bottom fabric, meshing the layers together.

Embellished fabric

Top left: Part-way through embellishing the fabric – see how the needles pull the fibres through, creating a slightly bumpy texture?

Top right: The finished embellished fabric, from the back. See how the fibres of the top fabric have been pulled through to the base fabric. This secures all the layers together.

Experimenting with the embellisher

- It is possible to take the embellishing process further to play with colour. For example, if your base fabric is black and all the surface colours are pale neutrals, if you turn the work onto the reverse side and embellish, the finished embellished surface on top will have tiny dark specks across the surface, made by the embellisher pulling the dark fabric layer through the fabrics. This creates more interest and texture.

- Once you have understood how layering works with the embellisher, it is then possible to play around with more layers to make incredibly textured works. For example, try putting a layer of a particular colour silk in between your two main fabric layers to deliberately create a soft blend of colours.

Layering silk over the fabric.

Appliqué

The name appliqué comes from the French verb *appliquer*, which translates as 'to attach' or 'to apply'. Needlework appliqué is a technique that is essentially just that: plain or decorative fabrics are cut into different shapes and patterns and are then sewn (or 'applied') onto a larger fabric base to form a picture or pattern. Appliqué is often used to decorate quilts, clothes and decorative panels, and is then finished with embroidery stitches made by hand or machine. You can also use the technique to repair a worn fabric, cutting it to a particular shape and applying it to the worn area as a decorative patch.

For my work, I use three different methods of appliqué: **simple onlay**, **broderie perse** and **hemmed**. Each one creates a slightly different effect in my designs.

Simple onlay appliqué

This is the simplest and most recognizable form of appliqué. The cut fabrics can be secured temporarily with pins and tacking/basting stitches before machine stitching. This technique is also known as raw-edge appliqué.

1 I begin by laying my small patches of fabric onto the fabric background. Don't worry if these patches have raw edges. Pin or tack/baste these in place.

2 Machine embroider the patches using free-motion embroidery, outlining their shape first and then adding detail if you wish.

House, cut out from pictorial print upholstery fabric.

Broderie perse appliqué

This is sometimes known as Persian embroidery. It was a very popular technique from the late-eighteenth to early-nineteenth centuries, as it was a way of reusing very expensive imported chintz fabric, a textile that was fashionable in this era. Motifs, such as flowers, leaves, trees and birds, were cut out and arranged onto a plain cotton fabric to create a new design, and then neatly stitched to the cotton base fabric to apply it. The design was then embroidered further, to give the applied fabric additional fine detail.

I love to use this technique in some of my work. My stash of vintage fabrics often features designs that depict detailed landscapes, animals or flora, and I cut these out to make them part of the scene I'm creating with my work.

To attach the appliqué shapes, I free-motion embroider over the main outlines in the design, then add a few hand stitches for further embellishment.

Hemmed appliqué

I use this technique if the applied shapes need to really stand out, as the stitches used for hemming (slip stitches) make the edge of the motif sit raised above the background.

This method is the same as a type of Indian appliqué – the first few steps show you how to create the flower shape that so often appears in Indian appliqué, but if you wish to make an alternative hemmed shape go straight to step 6.

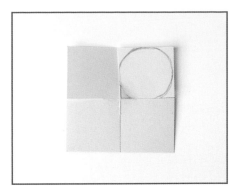

1 Fold a square of cartridge paper into quarters then open out. Draw a circle in one square, the edges of the circle touching the creases of the paper and the outer edges.

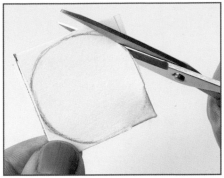

2 Refold the paper so only the circle is visible. Cut around three corners, leaving one corner on the fold uncut by a few millimetres (⅛in) or so.

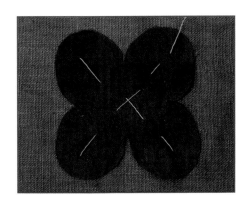

3 Lay the folded template over a piece of fabric folded into quarters – the centre of the fabric should be in the same corner as the uncut corner. Cut around the template.

4 Once the main shape is cut out, remove the template. In the uncut corner, cut only halfway into the folds of the fabric – don't cut all the way.

5 Unfold the fabric to reveal a symmetrical flower shape. This is a typical shape used in Indian appliqué.

6 Tack/baste the shape to your base fabric – make sure you tack/baste in a cross shape; this ensures the threads are away from the edges to be hemmed.

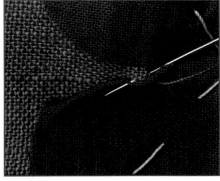

7 To hem, turn the edge of the fabric over by 4mm (⅛in) then take the threaded needle through the fold to hide the knot. Now take the needle through the base fabric and pick up a little of the edge of the appliqué shape – this is slip stitching.

8 Repeat this process all the way around the shape to hem.

Free-motion embroidery

At this stage, when all the main features of my work are in place, I begin the process of adding detail. This is the point where I outline any shapes in thread, or stitch in new ones completely. I want this part of the stitching to appear as if I have drawn onto the fabric with a pen.

For this reason, I sometimes like to call free-motion embroidery 'continuous line drawing': instead of using pencils and paper to draw, you get to use gorgeous fabrics and brilliant colourful threads! Free-motion embroidery is using your sewing machine to 'doodle' on your fabric to attach appliqué, or draw motifs and patterns across your fabric, or both! By adjusting the settings on your machine, and using a different sewing foot (a darning/free-motion foot), you are able to move freely over your fabric, thus allowing you to create flowing, unique details with your needle and thread. I mainly use free-motion machine embroidery as a means of putting detail on my cloths, alongside appliqué and hand stitching.

Continuous line drawing

The best way to develop skills in free-motion machine embroidery is to actually 'doodle'! Your sketchbook is a good place for this. To produce a continuous line drawing, simple draw without lifting the drawing instrument off the paper throughout the sketching process. This will mean that the pencil must move back and forth across the surface of the paper, with lines doubling back on each other, so that the drawing is one free-flowing, unbroken line.

If I need to draw a particular flower using free-motion embroidery, for instance, I like to begin by practising continuous line drawings of flowers in my sketchbook. This allows me to familiarize myself with the form of the flower, but also the movements needed to develop the drawing without lifting my pen or pencil from the paper. I do think that no matter how experienced you may be on the sewing machine, continuous line drawing on paper first is good practice when developing new work. It needn't take long, but it is time well spent!

Practise now with a pen and paper, playing with simple motifs to begin with: your name, flowers, fruit, a cup and saucer – anything that you can see from your table. Using a pen is key here – a pen means you can't erase any 'mistakes', and so will encourage you to not give up on your design. This will also allow you to build your creativity, develop your confidence and improve your drawing speed. Continuous line drawings work best when you try not to over think the process – just be spontaneous!

Continuous line drawing with a needle

Free-motion machine embroidery is like drawing with a sewing machine needle as you would a pen or pencil! In order to move freely over your fabric, you will need to make a few adjustments. Once these are set up, you are ready to go!

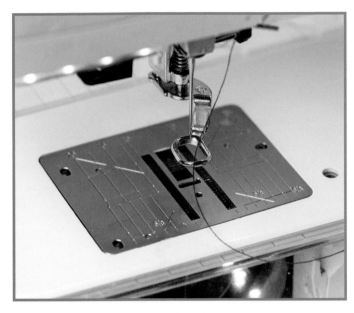

Setting up for free-motion embroidery

Ideally, a model of sewing machine with the ability to drop its feed dogs will make free-motion embroidery much easier (these are the teeth in the needle plate – see how they've been lowered?). You will then need to change your regular sewing foot for a darning/free-motion foot.

Example of free-motion embroidery in a stitched landscape.

See page 72 for the project.

- **Drop the feed-dogs in the machine** – This is the part of the machine that normally pushes fabric through the machine in a straight line. Dropping the feed-dogs may be a case of flicking a switch; some machines have a metal plate that has to be fitted; or, if you have a very old model, remove the foot and set the stitch length to '0'.
- **Set the stitch length to '0'** – This applies to all machines, new as well as old.
- **Change to a darning/free-motion foot** – There is a special foot you can buy and attach to the machine that doesn't grip the fabric like other feet do; this is called a darning or embroidery foot. It comes in various shapes and sizes, but the principle is the same: it has an open 'toe' – a hole in the foot of the needle that is either round or square in shape, and this enables you to see your stitching. The foot bounces up and down on the fabric, using a small spring, and this works to keep fabric flat as you stitch but without holding onto the fabric too much.
- **You don't need to use an embroidery hoop to steer with** – Personally, I prefer not to use a hoop: since my work is built up with layers of fabric, it tends to hold itself well under the machine. Saying that, if I were to free-motion embroider a fine fabric, such as silk, I would recommend stretching the fabric tightly in a hoop. Simply sandwich your fabric in between a hoop the wrong way round (i.e. the front of the fabric faces the inside hoop) and then hold on to the sides as you stitch!

What to do:

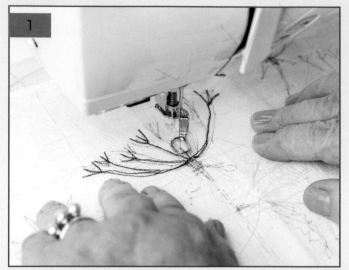

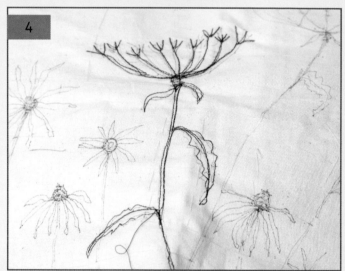

1 Lay your chosen fabric in place and set up your thread. Let's start with a plain calico. For most of my embroideries, I like to use either a grey or black thread as I want the stitching to look as though it has been drawn with a pen or pencil. Then, drop the foot lever and simply begin stitching. If you're new to free-motion embroidery, it helps to draw the design onto your fabric so you have lines to follow.

2 The best advice I can give is to put your foot down and go! You want the machine to be going fast, and sound fast; BUT, you are going to move the fabric around at your own speed. This way you will get a good stitched line.

3 Keep going! You will get better the more you stitch. If you have any areas that look really uneven, just stitch over them a second time. The two layers will blend and look much better.

4 Once the machine stitching is complete, snip off any loose threads; there is no need to fasten off.

TIP

If you have the machine going too slow, it can give the effect of larger stitches – not the look required, really. Of course, sewing fast means that straight lines are now really hard to do, and usually end up a little wobbly – this adds to the quirky nature of it all!

Experimenting

If your design features appliquéd fabric, you could leave the edges unhemmed and frayed, and then embroider over the top and around the outline of the shape. This secures the appliqué shape to the surface even more, and prevents the fabric from fraying further – but leaves enough of a frayed edge to create a textured effect.

Now let's embroider a more decorative background (see opposite). This is a ground fabric, and tacking/basting stitches have been used to assemble and combine an arrangement of fabric patches. With your drawing of choice as a reference, stitch as much of it as you can without stopping. You will have to double back on some lines, but this will create a drawn effect.

Close up of *Cow Parsley* **(see also page 86)**

In this piece, I have free-motion embroidered over fabric with an existing embroidered pattern, making the free-motion stitching look like foreground flowers in a meadow.

Free-motion embroidery is a very enjoyable, freeing process, and is something you'll soon get to grips with once you've become comfortable with the continuous flow of stitches. When you get stuck in, you'll find the possibilities really are endless!

By this stage, the whole surface of the cloth is secure, embellished down and details machine embroidered. The best bit of all is that I still have a soft, sumptuous cloth which the embellisher and all the machine stitching has softened even more!

We're now ready for the joy of hand stitching – the whole surface will be covered in myriad running stitches, French knots, couching stitches... Bliss.

Expressive hand stitches

Historically, certain embroidery stitches were used for very particular techniques, and how they were used and applied were almost wordlessly subscribed to by embroiderers: think goldwork, blackwork or traditional needlepoint. Stitches had to be very much considered and a perfect fit for the job.

Then came along teachers such as Rebecca Crompton and Constance Howard. These were embroidery rebels who said stitches can be used more freely, be uncomplicated, be expressive and break the rules. They encouraged a way of stitching that created lines, textures and marks in thread just as you would use a pencil or pen on paper.

The dictionary describes 'expressive' as conveying thought or feeling, a feeling that is meaningful, revealing, full of emotion, striking and artistic. This ideology that Crompton and Howard shared, and that I heartily advocate in my own work, is what I hope to inspire in your own designs as you follow the pages of this book. As an embroiderer, my needles and threads are my working media, and with them I can make marks just the same as an artist would with pens, pencils and a sketchbook.

However, in order to produce a contemporary approach to hand embroidery, we need to learn the rules in order to break them. In other words, it is important to understand 'stitches', research their traditional use, and then move forward and exploit them. With all the products on the market, and the novel techniques and quick fixes often advertised to us, we sometimes forget the stitch itself.

Every stitch has a particular quality and can be used expressively to create all sorts of marks, patterns and textures. My own favourite stitches, you'll see, are mostly simple line stitches that reflect the mark making of a pen or paintbrush. The stitch itself does not need to be difficult or complex; it's the expressive way it is used that creates the magic.

For this reason, avoid throwing a whole lot of stitches at a piece of work. This can actually be counterproductive, over-complicating a design and muddling the surface – especially when there are lots of layers of fabric that create a great deal of texture and interest already. Instead, try selecting a single stitch at first and exploit it throughout a whole piece of work; then build up to using a small selection that complement each other and the patterns you can see all over the background – two or three stitches are all you need.

When selecting stitches, don't forget that the same stitch can look completely different depending on the thickness of the thread, along with the size and direction of the stitch – hence why it is possible to work a single type of stitch across a whole composition. You may be able to wrap part of a stitch, or weave it in and out of another. Or you could pile the stitches on top of one another, all different sizes, to create scrumptious textures!

Consider your threads too, and select your appropriate colour palette. What will work best for your piece? A thread that is matt or shiny, and thick or fine? Very thick slubbed or knobbly threads are great for couching, as is garden twine and wire.

With the following collection of my favourite stitches, it is possible to create expressive and effective stitched surfaces.

Print & Stitch Sampler
25.5 x 25.5cm (10 x 10in)

The fabric was printed with a circle of sponge using acrylic paint. When dry, it was washed over with exhausted Procion® dye. The challenge was to hand embroider each circle with a different stitch or pattern.

Straight stitch

This creates lovely linear, cross-hatching or criss-cross effects, both formal and informal. A row of little straight stitches can create an effective square of needed detail, or when they are stitched with irregular lengths they can become grasses and distant hedgerows.

Seed

A lovely filling stitch – like scattered seeds, small straight stitches are made at different angles across a whole area with an almost random appearance.

Running stitch

Can be worked large and small. I use this stitch a lot to fill in my backgrounds, if worked in a single row it can give detail, or create a contrast of colour. I use it like darning stitch, making multiple rows of running stitches in all directions, as it gives a lovely ripple and movement to the surface and blends all my fabric patches and layers.

Couching

Great for thick lines, using threads like wools, bobbly, fluffy yarn, garden twine and wire; you can even use narrowly cut strips of fabric.

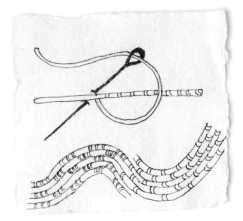

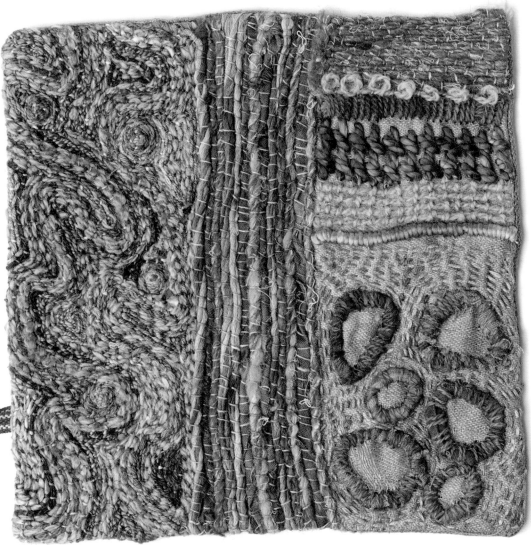

Couching stitch inspiration

· *Couching is a traditional stitch, once used to attach expensive and gold threads onto fabric. In this tradition, a finer thread was used to couch the ornate one, as in the central panel above.*

· *However, you can couch with the same thread to create texture, as in the green panel and the one above it.*

· *Try couching swirls (far left) and rings or circles (far right), not just in straight lines.*

Buttonhole stitch

This creates lovely rows of vertical lines, or spirals, circles or edgings. I love to use this stitch for creating shell forms for my work inspired by the sea.

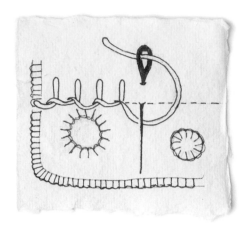

Buttonhole stitch inspiration

- Buttonhole stitch gives wonderful textures when worked randomly or in circles, and when layered over each other using various colours and thicknesses of thread.

- This stitch also creates strong linear shapes.

- Buttonhole stitch works very well as a couching stitch, especially when worked over thick threads, such as yarn, or strips of fabric.

- Buttonhole bars are traditionally used to make buttonholes or for cutwork. I like to use them to create a 'loose' bar–like shape that sits proud of the base fabric. When worked small, they almost look like bullion knots.

- Detached buttonhole stitch can be used to create a detached, lacey effect that almost looks like knitting.

Detached chain stitch

I love this stitch as a filling stitch, or worked in a ring to make wonderful little lazy-daisy flowers. It can also be wrapped to create chunky heavy stitches, and stitches can fit inside each other when creating texture.

Detached chain stitch inspiration

- This stitch makes a lovely lazy-daisy flower!

- It's also perfect as an alternative filling stitch, worked randomly over the surface – a bit like seed stitch (see page 54).

- In groups of three, as you can see in the top-left corner of this sampler, they will make a formal grid-like pattern.

- Use it to make lovely, intricately textured surfaces by piling stitches on top of each other, or making them fit inside another stitch – really pack them in! Using a range of different threads and thread thicknesses will make the effect greater.

- Use them for decorative couching.

Chain stitch

This makes excellent, chunky lines of stitching, and is perfect for creating outlines or more complex patterns or motifs in stitch. It can also be wrapped on top of itself to create chunky stitches, as the stitches can fit inside each other to create further texture. I sometimes distort the shape slightly, making them v- or square-shaped, or extending the length of the anchor stitch to create a leaf-like or stamen-like appearance.

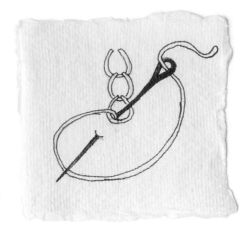

There is a look-alike stitch: raised chain band (worked in the left-hand centre of the sampler below). This is a composite stitch – a series of straight stitches are worked, then the chain is worked into the straight stitches. This stitch will also make a lovely chunky knot if worked as a detached stitch. It is an interesting stitch and worth investigating in a stitch dictionary. There are a whole range of chain stitch variations: rosette, twisted, cable, wheatear, whipped... and, of course, each variation has its variations! Have fun exploring.

Open chain

This stitch is great for linear texture, similar to chain stitch but with a square, ladder-like appearance (hence why it is sometimes known as 'ladder stitch'). This is also a variation of chain stitch.

Fly stitch

A lovely, organic stitch to create formal patterns or motifs, to use anywhere you may need a grid. Use complementary or harmonizing colours to define each row of the pattern.

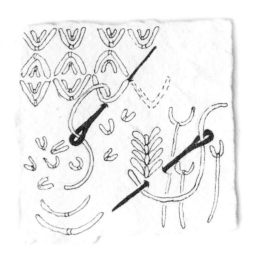

Fly stitch inspiration

- I use fly stitch mostly to create intricate little patterns, as the way the stitch is made allows greater flexibility for 'reshaping' the stitch.

- This is an excellent stitch for creating texture, and to use as a filling stitch.

- Layer and overlap fly stitches to form organic, natural shapes.

- Why not couch multiple fly stitches over a thicker thread to add further embellishment?

- Fly stitch can be worked with a longer anchor stitch to create a 'tail' – again, this helps to create successful patterns and motifs.

Knots

We think 'texture' when using knots, and French and bullion knots are certainly great at doing this! Bullion knots are particularly good for creating thick lines – almost like rows of little sausages or worms!

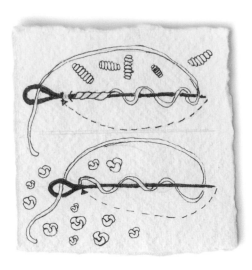

Knot stitch inspiration

· *French knots are perfect for giving elements of the design extra detail; for example, I use them to finish the heads of my beloved flower, cow parsley.*

· *Placing your bullion knots in rows can make a formal, grid-like pattern – excellent for filling an area of a design.*

· *Using a variety of threads and in different thicknesses and colours is especially effective with knot stitches – for example, a fine thread makes either knot wonderfully loose and loopy...*

Cretan stitch

My go-to stitch for textures! However, it can be used to make a formal pattern that's reminiscent of the details found in architecture, such as the example in the top left-hand corner of the sampler below.

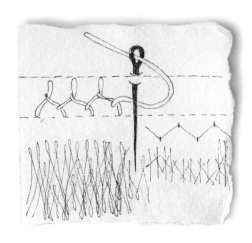

Cretan stitch inspiration

- Try layering the stitches in a wide range of threads, thickness and colours for different effects: on a small sample fabric, start with base-layer stitches made with thick threads; next, change the colour and use a slightly thinner thread. Continue changing colours and using finer threads with each layer, until a fine machine thread becomes the top layer.

- Cretan stitch is great for landscape scenes – especially making grasses.

- Wonderful, decorative circles can be formed with this stitch.

- Cretan stitch can be stretched out to look almost like a single line – as in the example in the top right-hand corner of the sampler below, within the wheel.

- The stitch can be made very short and stretched out to create textured yet linear effects – see the middle-left square.

RELAX INTO YOUR STITCHING

Yes, you will find hand stitching time consuming. If you understand that right from the beginning, my hope is that you'll discover that with it there is a quiet relaxation involved, a time to reflect and really begin to develop a connection with your work.

During the many years I taught City & Guilds courses, I always made a point of talking to students about self-discipline, and learning to be comfortable with sitting still and being at peace with a single activity. We live very busy lives, and everything seems to be running at a hundred miles an hour: a busy job, being a parent – or grandparent – looking after children or grandchildren; maybe you are looking after elderly relatives, flicking through social media, going shopping, cooking, doing housework... Phew! And as we're constantly rushing around, everything has to be a quick fix with even quicker results.

If it has been a long time – years perhaps – since you were able to spend any real time on a single project, it can be a very hard lesson to learn. So many times I have heard students tell me of a quicker option they'd like to take with their work: 'I am changing my mind and the design; it's going to take too long!' This is a shame. Trying to create an embroidery all too quickly will compromise the outcome, and you want the best outcome you can achieve.

When you are undertaking time-consuming work, try to embrace the process. Put on some of your favourite music or listen to audio books, or whatever works for you. I also like to sit with family or friends, or even watch TV while hand sewing.

I love the knowledge that I have a basket of sewing to relax into; it gives me a nice cosy feeling while I work, and I always look forward to it. By fully engaging with your work and enjoying the experience, you will find you're highly rewarded in both your skills and the final outcome.

'The greatest gift an artist has is not talent, but self–motivation.'
– David Millard, painter, 1918–2002

Historical & world sewing techniques

While I like to rely on contemporary methods of stitching my cloths to give them interest and detail, I also like to incorporate historical techniques in my work, as well as stitch methods found outside of Europe. Splicing these two together, in tandem with my expressive stitches, creates lovely, contemporary additions to small cloths.

Historical stitches

Crazy patchwork

Crazy patchwork rapidly became a national trend amongst urban, upper-class women of the Victorian period. The method involved piecing together hundreds of different little fabric pieces, using the wide variety of fabrics that the newly industrialized nineteenth-century textile industry offered. Long after the style had fallen out of fashion amongst urban women, it continued in rural areas and small towns, and the women there saw it as a way to share their embroidery and embellishment skills. The technique creates a highly embroidered and decorated surface, and – if simplified slightly – is a lovely addition to a cloth. I have used it to identify Venice in a small cloth (see page 100).

Close-up of one of my crazy-patchwork samplers, made in 1988.

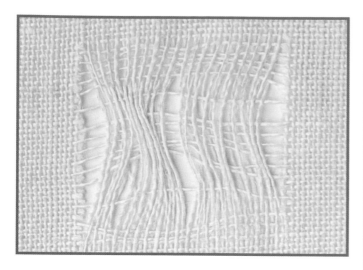

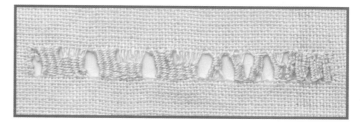

Drawn thread work

In the Victorian period, drawn thread work was used to transform evenly woven linen into delicate, lace-like fabric. They did this by drawing out sets of warp and weft threads in a piece of linen, and then working weaving stitches over the threads that remained. As threads are removed from the cloth, it is very important that you can count the threads in the linen. Traditionally, the technique was worked with white thread on white cloth, and mainly used to make decorative hems. After researching Beryl Dean's work, I found 'Fair Linen Alter Cloth, 1965' – a beautiful cloth made using drawn thread work. As a little homage to Beryl Dean, I produced a small piece of drawn thread work, worked in a more contemporary way using hand-dyed fabric and thread. I then integrated this small sample into a small cloth inspired by Venice; it fitted perfectly with the theme of grids I had been exploring (see page 104).

World stitches

Indian appliqué

One type of Indian appliqué, explained on page 47, involves folding a square of fabric into four and cutting a symmetrical shape through all the layers. This technique was used for the yellow flowers in the sample, left. Another popular Indian technique is a form of reverse appliqué, where the top layer is cut away to reveal the fabric underneath. This technique was used for the two red bands in the sample, left. I used both techniques in my memory cloth on page 104.

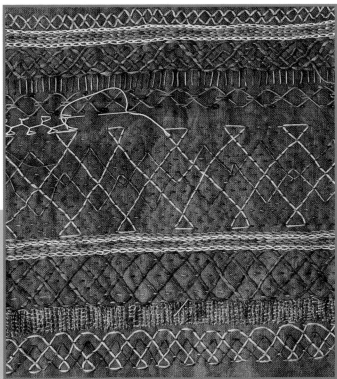

Banjara quilting

This is a method practised by the nomadic tribes of the northern plains of India. It uses the running stitch and interlacing that I have explored as part of my Venice work. Changing the colours to my own colour palette, the grid-like effect it produces is simply wonderful.

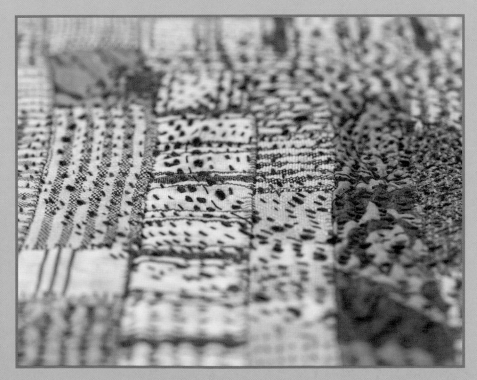

Kantha

Kantha is a type of quilting/embroidery technique worked traditionally in Bangladesh. Bengali women overlap old saris and hand-stitch them together to make a thin piece of quilted cloth. Calico is also used instead of old sari fabric to make a simpler cloth. The whole surface of the fabric is quilted using just a running stitch, worked in close rows, straight lines, meandering lines and circles – the latter two often stitched around existing embroidered patterns or pattern darning. The rows of stitching create a lovely ripple effect on the surface of the cloth.

Experimental embellishments

When we talk about embellishing textiles we usually mean beads and sparkle. I like to take a more experimental approach and most of the time prefer to use my collections and findings.

Beachcombing is one of my favourite activities. I have a huge collection of glass, ceramics, shells, rusty metal pieces, flattened beer-bottle tops, feathers, twigs and found objects, all of which make great embellishments for my work. The whole process of collecting is so pleasurable. On returning home, objects may need washing then are carefully stored in my lovely vintage tins, baskets and boxes. It really has become an obsession! Family and friends are bemused when I have to double back to pick up some obscure object, something I probably can't live without!

Embellishments are used in a variety of ways across my body of work when appropriate, from formal pieces like my stitched landscapes and memory cloths to smaller samplers. Mostly, I just use smaller pieces of vintage ephemera, such as buttons or old jewellery, to decorate these works. However, a whole piece (such as the one on the opposite page) can be made using objects collected during dog walks in woodlands and on beaches – sea glass, beach ceramics, feathers, twigs etc. Below are my most common embellishments.

Feathers

When out on our dog walks I cannot resist picking up feathers! But for a while, I didn't really know what to do with them. After experimenting in my sketchbook I found that they are great for couching, and I work stitches along the central spine of the feather: first, I cut all the feathers to the same length, trimming off the nib at the bottom of the feather. As I couch them down I turn them alternately, which produces a herringbone pattern with a linear quality, and an interesting colour, texture and pattern.

Sea glass & ceramics

I often find sea glass and ceramics on the beach that have been softened and rounded by the sea. I use a thick, sticky glue to apply them to fabric then, when dry, I completely stitch over the surface using a random, cross-hatching of straight stitches.

Pebbles

Tiny pebbles are applied and stitched over like sea glass and ceramics; however, they sit better on a heavy-weight fabric, such as canvas, which can take the weight.

Twigs

Small twigs are lovely to introduce to a couched panel, and are an abstract way to depict the undulations and rhythms of a landscape. Cut them into small pieces and couch over them to form patterns – herringbone or a simple grid – using interesting threads.

Driftwood

Larger pieces are collected to be used for presentation. My husband kindly and expertly cuts the wood into appropriately sized pieces then sands, waxes and polishes them for me. Three-dimensional birds made of fabric sit on little round wooden plinths/bases and similarly made bird heads are mounted onto flat pieces of driftwood. Small pieces I stitch into sketchbooks and onto fabric samples, and little woven experiments.

Industrial items (bottle tops, washers, etc.)

Rusty beer-bottle tops that have been flattened can be glued and stitched to work. Flat simple washers stitched into place also create patterns and add form.

A Walk on the Beach
No.1 in the series. 46 x 51cm (18 x 20in)

*This piece was hand-dyed initially. Small circular shapes cut from silk, both plain
and patterned, were applied using free-motion embroidery. Shells, sea glass and
pebbles were then stitched on by hand. A piece of driftwood, woven to the fabric
with hand-dyed thread, hangs from the bottom edge.*

Taxidermy eyes

Taxidermy eyes give the larger birds a more realistic look and a glint in the eye! These eyes are made of glass and are beautifully painted to match a particular bird's eyes exactly. I use a range of sizes to match the bird I am making – 4mm, 6mm, 10mm and 12mm. There are several websites that supply taxidermy eyes. I prefer the eyes that have a wire coming out from the back of the eye. It may be necessary to order more than one size at first to determine the size you need.

Beads

I tend to use coloured glass beads to embellish appliqué motifs, mainly to create the eyes for animals (usually birds!) on my landscape cloths. You can find small beads in many shops, brick and mortar or online. Choose whichever size suits the animal or perspective of your piece.

Craft and florist's wire

For forming the legs, feet and wings of the birds (see also pages 119–121, 124 and 125).

Buttons

I especially love the buttons that have come from my Mum's old button box – those delightful little vintage cloth buttons and glass buttons. I particularly like buttons that have come from industrial clothing like overalls and very old boots, which have little metal loops at the back. I have used buttons on my memory cloth pieces; they add detail and punctuate an empty space. I have made a lovely memory cloth in remembrance of my Mum, worked in a grid design, using lots of lovely treasured buttons and little silver buckles from her precious button tin (see page 101).

Using taxidermy eyes and florist wire for my bird sculpture, Woody the Wood Pigeon. See page 130 for more information on this piece.

Expressive projects

Embarking on a new project, how exciting! All the visual material has been gathered, and the experimental development of ideas has been worked in your sketchbook. You are ready to get started.

This section of the book takes you through the making of three possible projects – a stitched landscape, a memory cloth or a three-dimensional bird. My own sketchbook development has taken me to this point, too – by now you'll have had lots of possible compositions, colour schemes, textures and stitch solutions, suggestions of the written word maybe, drawings of birds, collections of wood for presentation… a total exploration of your creativity.

I would like to emphasize at this point that you can follow the step-by-step instructions to the letter if you want to, but I hope you are able to use your own inspirational ideas and put your own stamp on your work. For example, my landscape is square; yours could be wide and narrow, or maybe a series of small squares that hang together. Your memory cloth could be quite a lot bigger, to fold and lay over the back of a chair or hang as a statement piece at the head of the bed; most dramatic of all, it could be quilt sized! Your birds can become a little more unrealistic and fantastical, an approach that is particularly suitable if you're entirely new to sewn sculptures.

Don't worry about breaking rules, just be expressive and enjoy the process. I hope my work inspires you to make your own unique creations.

Stitched Landscape

Living so close to the Lincolnshire Wolds in the UK, a beautiful range of valleys and hills, means I can regularly drive through undulating, rolling landscapes. It's incredibly magical and always draws me in! The rows of trees on the skyline, mesmerizing hedgerows full of cow parsley, grasses, May blossoms and ancient hedging... The whole scene has so much to offer in terms of inspiration. First there are the sumptuous and varied colours – there is an overwhelming array of purples, greens, acid yellows from the rapeseed fields, greys, pinks, oranges and browns. Then there are the other design elements – textures, lines, forms and shapes blooming from flowers, fields, fences, trees and the little cottages. It's no wonder that the countryside and nature are such amazing inspirational sources.

I like to spend time drawing in the landscape and funnily enough, unlike many artists these days, I don't work from photographs. I don't want to create a realistic landscape – a photograph can do that. Taking elements of what I see and mixing them up a bit captures a landscape that expresses the mood and experience I have taken away from seeing the real thing. For example, my colour approach to landscape is not always realistic, simply my own interpretation. Applying shapes to the landscape adds form, context and detail, and finally stitching adds the texture. Detail gives strength to the work and anchors everything together.

As well as creating a landscape piece that, to some extent, depicts an actual scene in fabric and stitch, a landscape design could also be represented in a more abstract or unusual way. Here are some options that I like to use in my own work:

- compose a bird's eye view of the landscape;
- incorporate maps of the location in the work itself, forming the scene in a more interesting and connected way;
- create multiple hedgerow or tree motifs, inspired by those captured on location, to form a border on a landscape cloth;
- change the scale or the view – this is simplifying to the extreme!
- make the landscape using a combination of actual items collected from the place, which you stitch or embellish over – the landscape as such is lost, but the items in the piece work to depict the place instead, creating a much more interesting, abstract suggestion of the scene.

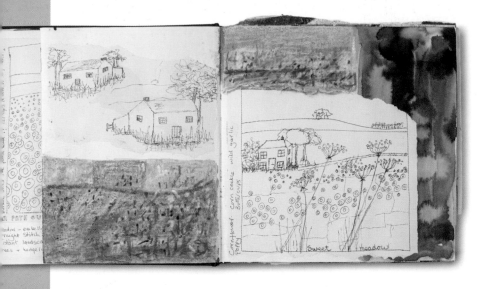

Developing a stitched landscape

Getting all the components of your landscape in place will rely heavily on your sketchbook drawings, and a simple plan. We touched briefly on developing your initial drawings to prepare a design (see page 34). For more pictorial pieces of work, such as a stitched landscape, you will need to consider several additional factors at this final drawing stage.

Perspective is a very important one, as this will help convey the scene you wish to depict more 'realistically' in a more expressive, abstract way. For example, note early on how colours become paler as you work from the bottom and up to the horizon line (except when it's a dark, stormy sky), and any detail almost disappears around this area too – this is called aerial perspective. Conversely, richer and darker colours, as well as any bold details and texture, should appear strongly at the bottom edge of your composition – the foreground – to suggest its closeness to the viewer. You will see more details, too, and this is a prime place to add any embellishments you considered early on in your sketchbook.

Note also any key elements from the scene – is there a particular plant or building that has caught your eye? Or maybe there are creatures or birds that seem to be in abundance? These are useful things to highlight and have as focal points in your picture, and will help to give it more purpose and structure.

I like to think of a landscape as a series of horizontal 'layers' of colour and texture. It is then punctuated by vertical lines of growth – grasses, flowers, trees and hedgerows. Once these are in place, you can use them as guides for where to place your details, such as buildings, detailed flowers or animals.

When your plan is in place, and your base fabric prepared, select a range of fabrics in your appropriate colour scheme. Again, remember perspective but also think about textures. Fabrics can include hand-dyed cottons, linens, silks, recycled embroidered cloths, sari silks and patchwork cottons, and these can be dyed with cold-water dyes or even stained with tea or coffee. Some fabrics may require printing or stencilling.

- **Approximately 40cm (15in) square of fabric, for the base:** this can be adjusted if you have decided to go for your own composition. If you want to join two pieces of fabric for the base, do not seam them together as it will create bulk; we are trying to create a lovely soft surface to stitch. Just simply overlap both edges of the fabric then tack/baste them together; this may feel a bit unpractical, but there will be so much stitching in the fabric later, it will become very secure eventually.

- **Appropriate-sized strip of fabric, for the sky:** alternatively it could be layers of smaller pieces of fabric; the sky doesn't have to be a solid strip.

- **Scraps of different types and shades of fabric, for the meadow:** using the finished design on page 73, or based on your own drawings and sketchbook workings, select a variety of fabrics in different colours – saying that, make sure that they tonally work together. If you wish, as I have done, you can dye a few of the fabrics to make the piece more cohesive.

- **Scraps of white, green, orange and blue fabrics, for the foreground flowers, leaves and grass**

- **Merino wool tops in light brown, yellow, light green and dark green, for the trees**

- **Dark grey, brown and green machine threads**

- **Variety of embroidery threads:** I have used a combination of green, cream, beige, turquoise, gold and hand-dyed threads

- **Stitching tools (see page 12),** with the exception of the embellisher

- **Optional:** you may decide to add a building to your landscape, such as a cottage or barn. If you can find a furnishing fabric with a little cottage, cut it out and it can be added to your work with broderie perse (see page 46). Alternatively, make a little cottage by drawing one onto a piece of calico, painting it, cutting it out and then applying it to your piece.

Preparing your base

1 Begin with the base fabric. Select a nice soft fabric – I used recycled linen or cotton. It can be the size and shape of your choice, and more than one piece of fabric can be joined if you do not have a big enough piece. There is no need to seam the base fabrics together – simply overlap and tack/baste together in place to avoid any bulk.

2 Gather all your fabrics that will build your landscape. Tear strips and large squares from them, rather than cutting with scissors – it gives the shapes a much softer edge. Tear some of these strips into smaller squares and rectangles.

3 Once you have lots of blocks of fabric, begin to lay them out over the base fabric. Use your sketchbook plan to help you at this stage; generally, I tend to work from the top down and ensure that each block is slightly overlapping the others. Besides creating a lovely linear, abstract effect across the whole piece, this will make the fabric more secure later.

Appliqué

4 Once the main landscape blocks are tacked/basted in place, add in the broderie perse cottages or country buildings (see the photo on page 46 and the photo, left, for help). Remember the importance of perspective here – the size of your own buildings will determine where they should sit in your composition. As my mine were quite small, I placed them around the top of the meadow, near the 'horizon line'.

5 Using the cottages as a reference for sizing, cut out your onlay appliqué flora from your scraps of flower and leaf fabric. Note that the petals of the daisies and bellflowers, and the leaves, are the only pieces I've placed at this point – the main 'petals' of the cow parsley, the grass stems and centres of the daisies will be machine sewn on later, during the free-motion embroidery stage.

6 Tack/baste all the surfaces onto the base fabric to secure them in place temporarily.

Back of the fabric, once all the elements have been tacked/basted in place.

TIP

Spray adhesives and iron-on fusible webbing products are available to hold down applied decorative bits of fabric. However, they conflict with the natural, organic nature of the materials used. I prefer not to use them; tacking/basting is a much more favoured technique. The fabric remains soft and pliable this way, making it lovely to hold and stitch.

Free-motion embroidery

7 Take your sewing machine and set it up for free-motion embroidery (see also pages 48–50). Begin with the cottages at the top of your piece: with the dark grey machine thread, embroider over the main outlines – the building itself, the roof, the windows and the door.

8 Change to a brown machine thread and embroider tree trunks either side of the cottage – note how the right-hand tree is larger, because it is closer to the foreground.

9 Pull off thin lengths of yellow, brown and light green fibre from your selection of merino wool tops and tease them into each other to create a variegated green ball. Lay the ball over the top of one tree trunk. For a nice bit of contrast and to convey the idea that the right-hand tree is in shadow, pull off and tease together lengths of fibre only from the light and dark green merino wool tops for the canopy of the other tree. With green thread in your sewing machine, embroider over the fibres here and there – don't overdo it, as you want to keep some of their texture and dimensionality for realism. As you embroider the fibres, use your fingers to move them around a little to ensure you create the tree canopy shape desired. Once the tree canopies are sewn in place, rough up the stitched fibres with the blunt end of a hand-sewing needle, so that the stitches aren't too dominant.

10 Now for the onlay appliqué. Switch back to the dark grey thread and free-motion embroider around the petals of one of the daisies. Embroider around the edge of each petal a few times for a sketchy effect. It's not imperative to secure the appliqué petals entirely – you want the edges to be slightly loose to give them movement and realism.

11 Take an orange circle and place it over the centre of the daisy, then embroider all around a few times to secure it in place.

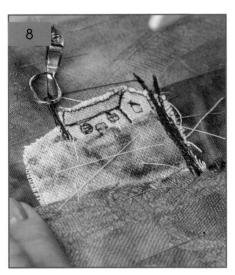

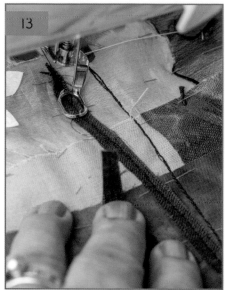

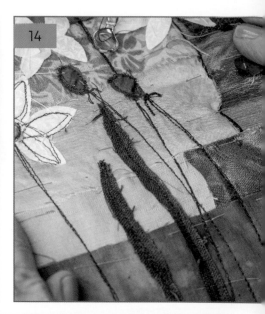

12 Between two daisy petals, start to embroider a stem and sew all the way down to the bottom edge of your piece. Work up and down several times to create a relatively thick stem.

13 If desired, grab one of your cut grass stems and lay it slightly over the stem just stitched. If you wish, criss-cross a few stems a little, for some realism. Use the same process to stitch the grasses in place – sew up and down several times, and work mainly along the centre of the grass stems to give the edges of the fabric some movement.

14 For some of the onlay appliqué leaves, draw in the stems using free-motion machine embroidery, then stitch around the leaves a couple of times to secure in place.

15 Continue to free-motion embroider the remaining onlay appliqué motifs in the same way, alternating between each type of flora to ensure the stems and flowers criss-cross over one another as realistically as possible.

To make the bell flowers [**A**], use either the brown or dark grey thread to stitch creases into the centres of the flower shapes and around the base – leave the tops loose and frayed for effect. For their stems, embroider them in place using the same technique as the daisy stems. As you can see, hand stitches will be worked over them later for further texture.

For the cow parsley [**B**], establish the stem initially with dark grey thread then immediately lay on the head shape at the top end and embroider to secure. Note I've followed the curves of the parsley head, swinging left to right to create smaller and smaller U-shapes as I work upwards, and ending each 'U' with tiny spikes. Once the fabric is secured, snip into the edges of the tops of the parsley heads a little with small sharp scissors, to deliberately fray them and add a little texture.

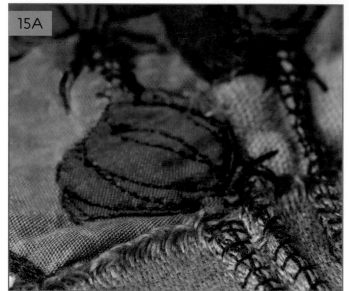

Expressive hand stitches

16 Hand stitching not only neatens up any free-motion embroidered elements in the piece, but it pulls it all together – especially if you are using only a selection of stitches.

Begin with the background – the meadow and sky blocks. These are stitched with running stitches. Depending on the colour fabric you are working on, use either variegated, hand-dyed threads, or green, gold and cream threads. Pale, cream and blue threads suit the sky; the greener and more gold hues suit the meadow.

In addition, for each block, try to change the direction of the running stitches; for example, if one block of meadow has been stitched horizontally, running from left to right, make the stitches in the next block run vertically.

For the sky, which is one long length of fabric, you can make 'blocks' with the stitches to mirror the block stitching below in the meadow.

TIP

Hand-dyeing your threads at the same time as the fabric is not only time saving, it helps to create more harmony in your final composition; as the threads and fabrics are dyed with the same colours, tonally they will complement each other very effectively.

17 For the cottage at the top of the horizon line, work straight stitches in green thread in front of and behind some sections of the building to make grasses. Embroider little seed stitches in the trees using variegated thread.

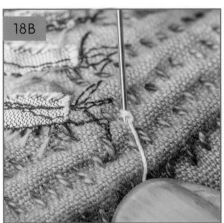

18 To finish off the cow parsley heads, embroider French knots all along the tops with either cream or white embroidery thread. To make a French knot, begin by bringing the threaded needle up through the fabric close to the desired spot. Wrap the thread around the tip of your needle twice [**A**]. Holding onto the working thread with your non-working hand, insert the needle into the desired spot [**B**], close to where you came up. As the needle goes through the fabric, keep holding onto the thread to maintain a little tension. When almost all the working thread has been pulled through, let go – it will slip through the knot and finish it off. Repeat to cover each cow parsley head [**C**].

19 To create the effect of anthers and finish off the bellflowers, embroider several pistil stitches along the top raw edges with turquoise thread [**A**]. Pistil stitches are made similarly to French knots, except the point at which you insert the wrapped needle is further away from the point you came up.

To give the stems of the bellflowers a spiky, three-dimensional appearance, pinch the fabric along the free-motion embroidered stem then work overcast stitches all the way down with dark brown embroidery thread [**B**].

Finishing off

20 Once the whole surface of your embroidery is covered in stitches, the cloth is complete. Remove all tacking/basting stitches. To create a neat edge all around, turn under each edge of the fabric by 6mm (¼in) or so, pinning if needed. Secure the hem with hem stitch: thread the needle (I am using variegated embroidery thread and an embroidery needle), tie a knot at the end and then bring the needle up through the crease in the fold to start – this will hide the knot. Take the needle through a little of the unfolded fabric, close to the hemmed edge, then bring it out through the folded fabric. Pull gently to create the first stitch. Repeat all around.

Making a meadow

A combination of onlay appliqué, free-motion embroidery and hand stitching, and criss-crossing the different flowers, gives a fantastic variety of texture and interest, and creates some realism in this otherwise abstract composition.

Landscape with a Bird
35.5 x 40.5cm (14 x 16in)

Inspiration for this piece of work came from driving through the Lincolnshire Wolds. I love the gentle roll of the hills, with little cottages nestled in. A garden bird and the native daisy has become a bold, exaggerated foreground. Linen was used as the base fabric. A range of vintage and hand-dyed fabrics were then arranged on top. The techniques I used include onlay appliqué, broderie perse and free-motion embroidery. Almost all of the cloth's surface was darned with variegated thread. A turned hem finished the piece.

Landscape – Meadow
38 x 40.75cm (15 x 16in)

I am always inspired as we drive through the Lincolnshire Wolds. On one drive we suddenly came across a beautiful meadow – stop the car! I needed to take in the view. Since then I became quite obsessed with finding new meadows. A visit to Helmsley Walled Garden in North Yorkshire, UK, had a whole section of the garden turned to meadow – it was spectacular. Cow parsley filled the hedgerows and became the foreground of this work.

Again, linen was the base fabric for this piece. A selection of vintage and hand-dyed fabrics were used for the main landscape. A combination of broderie perse and onlay appliqué was used. Free-motion embroidery added details to the appliqué shapes. Most of the meadow section was hand embroidered, featuring French knots, straight stitches and darning stitches. In addition, wool fibres were added for the trees, secured with hand stitching. The edges were finished with a turned hem.

Two Hares in a Landscape
48.25 x 48.25cm (19 x 19in)

Driving to my daughter's cottage on top of the Lincolnshire Wolds, there are lovely little roads that meander off the beaten track. Fields flank these small country roads, and as we drive down the lanes we've seen hares in the fields a few times. They are beautiful creatures and are very inspirational – hence why they sit perfectly in my landscape!

For the base fabric I used linen. Vintage fabrics including silk, cotton lace, broderie anglaise, wool and hand-dyed hessian were torn and placed across the whole fabric. Appliqué accents include broderie perse (for the hares) and onlay appliqué for the foreground leaves. These were outlined and embellished with free-motion embroidery. Hand stitches such as straight stitch, lazy-daisy stitch, couching and darning/running stitch were worked across most of the piece. A turned hem was applied around the cloth at the end.

Beachscape – Egret
38 x 35.5cm (15 x 14in)

One of our favourite walks is along a coastal path in Lincolnshire, from Humberston to Tetney. Part of the walk takes in the Tetney Marshes – a nature reserve and bird sanctuary. There are sand dunes that form a salt marsh, tall grasses, meadow flowers and small areas of water – it is stunning. It's a wonderful place to visit, especially if you enjoy the birds: we have been watching a pair of egrets for about five years as we walk Bertie our dog.

This piece features layers of hand-dyed fabrics on a linen ground. Appliqué features include broderie perse and onlay appliqué; the egret's legs and beak were made with a fine black leather. The egret's head was completed with a black glass bead for the eye. A printed word was also added and framed with hand stitching. Stitching accents include free-motion embroidery, straight stitches and darning stitches. The abstract edges of this piece were neatened, emphasized and finished with a turned hem.

Cow Parsley
25.5 x 124.5cm (10 x 49in)

When out walking with Bertie in a local ancient woodland, we took a narrow pathway through a magical area full of cow parsley. The flowers stood on both sides of the path, towering over our heads at about 183- to 213-centimetres (6- to 7-foot) tall. I had to go back several times to take it all in, as it was as if we had wandered into a fairy dell! I spent time sketching the scene, and eventually developed this tall towering piece of work depicting these wonderful flowers.

There is a pieced linen base, with hand-dyed vintage embroidered cloths torn and arranged over the top. Cow parsley features were made 'simply' through free-motion machine embroidery and topped with French knots. The whole surface was then darned completely using hand dyed threads, with a turned hem to finish.

Meadow Landscape with Two Hares
46 x 43cm (18 x 17in)

This is part of a series of works that I produced in response to meadows and hares. This time, the meadow has taken centre stage in the foreground.

This piece features a linen base topped with a range of hand-dyed fabrics. The bottom of the piece – the 'meadow of flowers' – was made initially with circles of silk, which were then secured with free-motion embroidery. Straight stitches, worked using a combination of wool and embroidery

threads, formed the flower petals. The hares are onlay appliqué, cut from felt, stuffed slightly before being secured in place on the cloth, then outlined and detailed with hand stitching. Glass bead eyes complete them. Other hand stitches in the piece include detached chain stitch and seed stitch. Wool fibres were applied for the trees. The edges were finished with a turned hem.

Memory Cloth

' The human hand allows the mind to reveal itself.'
– Maria Montessori, physician and educator, 1870–1952

Memories are one of the main sources of inspiration for my work, and I try to find ways of connecting memories to cloth. These can be memories of a place, a person or journey. I like to fully immerse myself in my inspirational sources when making a cloth like this, collecting and creating as many materials as I can to use later in my work.

I hope this section of my book will encourage you to embark on, almost quite literally, a 'creative journey'. Select your theme or memory. It could be a special place, a holiday, a memory of a special person in your life, an event or even a favourite walk. Once your memory has been chosen, take some time happily collecting all your evidence – photographs, sketches, bits and pieces of ephemera. Use these to inspire motifs or textures – the 50-square grid on page 31 is perfect for this process – and then find ways to unify all the different elements together to design a harmonious cloth. This could be through colour, using the same stitch to create details in another section of the cloth, or simply allowing the expressive hand stitching at the end to pull everything together.

One of the greatest aspects of this project is that it permits you to use a range of recycled fabrics, which are especially important if they are connected in some way to your own special memory. As described before, dyeing is an excellent way of making sure all your different recycled fabrics harmonize nicely.

There is a combination of techniques that we can explore and think about before we start our stitched memory. Ask yourself: is your cloth going to be rich in colour and embellishment? Or does it need to be simple and naïve? Whichever direction you choose, for me it is very important when stitching a cloth that the whole experience feels comfortable and enjoyable. There is a need within me to connect with the cloth. More often than not, taking a simple approach enhances the wonderful activity of stitching.

Use the following pages to find inspiration for your own work. I would love my book to encourage you to make your own small memory cloth. I strongly advocate a slow-stitch approach to this design, as this belongs to the experience of reliving the memory of your place or person.

89

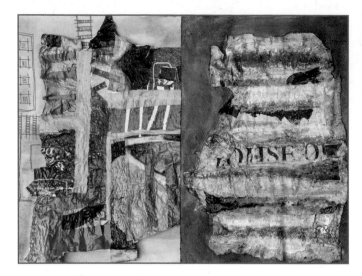

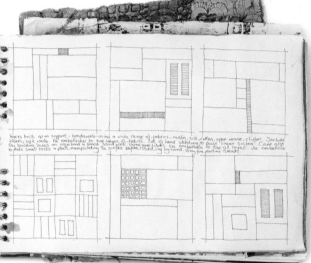

Developing a memory cloth

After travelling to different places around the world, recording and collecting what I'd seen and found in my sketchbooks, I decided to make a series of 'memory cloths'.

I have found Venice in Italy to be the greatest source of inspiration for my memory cloths. Venice is full of the most wonderful architecture, rich with ornate detail: the designs of the gates, doors, windows, shutters and grilles are deceptively simple, and they also seem to be made in every type of material – wood, metal, stone and more – and each one is similar in their beauty and intricacy. The decaying grandeur of the place, with its peeling paint, water-stained walls and faded colours, is fascinating to me. In contradiction to the old architecture I admired, I found I also loved the contemporary graffiti I saw everywhere, and the torn and peeled billboards against all the aged opulence.

After several visits, I decided to record the city's architecture as small grids within my sketchbook, using the grids as a way of zooming in on particular features and textures that, for me, captured the faded beauty of the city. Grids were a natural form for me to use and help me focus in on these elements of Venice for my memory cloths, as these squares in themselves were memories – it was a technique created by my mum and me during my childhood when we used to draw grids together.

Through these grids, my sketchbook work has explored the features of Venice using different mixed media. I have used oil pastels and ink (great for quick expressive marks and colour), collage (to suggest the range of textures and surfaces I saw) and used ageing and distressing techniques to develop the overall colour palette for the piece. To reflect the graffiti and more modern elements of the Venice I saw, I decided to include words in some of my other Venice memory cloths, as I knew I wanted to print and hand embroider meaningful words on both the papers and fabric that would eventually form part of the work.

Preparing your base & appliqué

3

1 Begin with your square of base fabric, the right side facing down. Tear up or roughly cut out your larger block elements from your scraps of fabric. You can use the final design on page 89 to help you; otherwise, this is where the planning in your sketchbook is essential: it will ensure that you cut the 'correct' scraps of fabric, and at the right size.

Once all the large blocks are cut out, arrange them on your base fabric.

2 Again, referring to either the finished design on page 89 or your sketchbook, cut out the smaller shapes from your scrap fabrics with a small, sharp pair of scissors – these could be little squares and circles cut from cotton, or tiny rectangular shapes cut from felt.

3 When all your smaller shapes are cut out, begin to lay them onto their appropriate blocks. Use your sketchbook plan to help you at this stage, but if some areas prove too busy or sparse, feel free to change things a little to ensure a balanced piece. As with the Stitched Landscape (see page 72), overlapping different elements not only creates a wonderful abstract effect, it makes the fabric more secure – essential, as most of this design is stitched by hand.

When you are happy with your layout, tack/baste all the elements to the base fabric with machine thread.

4 To help pull all the different elements in the design together, and 'knock back' some of the bolder shades seen in some of the blocks, lay a large square of black chiffon over the top of your whole design. If necessary, pin the chiffon in place. Of course, you can use a different colour of chiffon if preferred.

Embellishing

5 As there are lots of little components to this cloth, I used the embellisher to secure them to the base fabric. This means no machine stitching is needed, allowing the hand stitches later to stand out much more. The embellisher creates a little bit of texture in the blocks as well.

Operate the embellisher just as you would with a sewing machine on a free-motion embroidery setting – move the fabric around as you press the foot pedal to felt the layers together. Embellish the whole cloth, over the chiffon, to secure all your layers together.

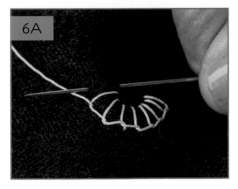

6A

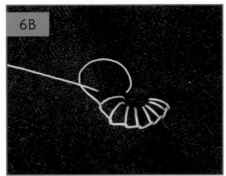

6B

6C

Expressive hand stitches

Hand stitches are one of the key features of a memory cloth. Machine-stitched words, sewn onto a narrow tape, are applied to some cloths, but not often.

6 To begin, I'm going to stitch a row of buttonhole wheels – they fit nicely in a long, narrow panel. This design feature, for me, is reminiscent of architectural details I saw in Venice. I have used cream, burgundy and turquoise thread. You can use a round object and a sharp pencil to mark out circles as a guide for stitching. Then, work buttonhole stitch in a circle to create the wheel.

7 Continue to make several more buttonhole wheels within the same panel – I made nine wheels overall. With each wheel, you can use a different colour thread. When all the wheels were stitched, I worked a straight stitch in between each wheel using grey embroidery thread. The panel was finished by stitching a French knot at the centre of each wheel, using the same grey thread for cohesion.

8 Seed stitch is a lovely stitch to fill an element or to use as a filling stitch to work around other shapes. I'm filling a whole panel with stitches here, but you may wish to use seed stitch to create pattern, or to fill in some of your own motifs. See page 54 for more on seed stitch.

Finished panel of buttonhole wheels.

8

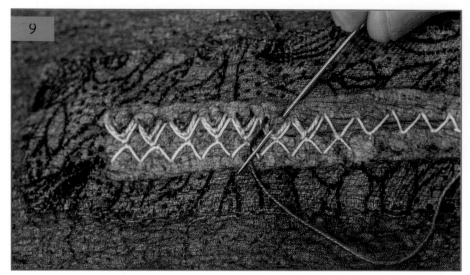

9 When I was in Venice, I found little bits of architectural detail that were reminiscent of diamond shapes. Fly stitch is perfect for creating little blocks of pattern like this. Using a range of threads in complementary colours, build rows of fly stitch – your pattern can be as long or as wide as you need to fit in one of the panels or blocks on your cloth. (Instructions and inspirational ideas for fly-stitch variations are on page 59.)

10 To complete the fly-stitch pattern and to fill the centre row of diamonds developed from the previous rows, work a row of fly stitch – shown in the orange, thicker thread – down the middle. These fly stitches will sit sideways in relation to the previous rows. If you wish, why not sew a small glass bead in between each fly stitch? Darning stitch/running stitch has been worked into the surrounding yellow and black fabric to finish the panel; this gives a lovely ripple texture and ensures the patch is secured to the base fabric.

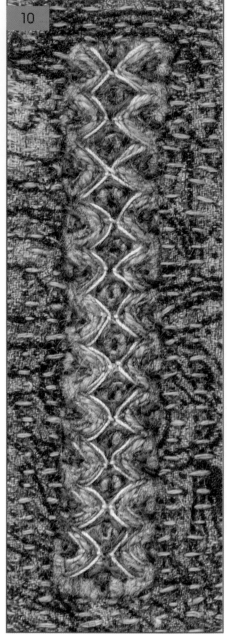

11 To allow the patterned fabric to shine through a little more, you can cut away some of the black chiffon. Feel free to do this in other sections of the cloth also, before adding your background running stitches – either across the whole panel or even just in a few spots – if you feel that the fabric needs more vibrancy.

12 One feature I couldn't help but notice throughout my trips to Venice was the numerous shutters on windows and doors I saw throughout the city! For this reason, I was determined to incorporate the ridged texture of the shutters in my memory cloth. For demonstration purposes, I am using a different fabric panel and alternative-coloured threads in the next three steps, just to show you how diverse the results can be.

Begin by pinching the very edge of your chosen panel with your fingertips; then, still holding the pinched fabric in place, work overcast stitches all the way along [A]. Repeat the process at the centre of the panel, then again at the other edge of the panel, to create three ridges [B].

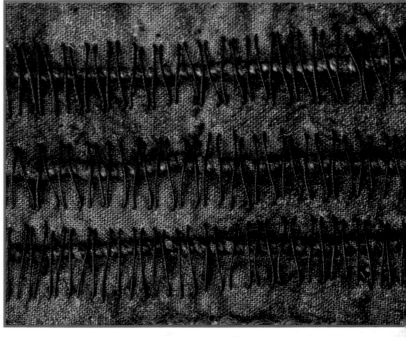

13 Over the stitched folds of fabric and using a different-coloured thread, work ladder stitch – these are reminiscent of the 'slats' on the shutters.

The 'couched' ladder-stitched panel in the final cloth. See how using different threads changes the impact of the stitches – in the finished piece, I used hand-dyed threads to overcast stitch each pinched fabric line.

95

14A

14B

14 To echo the ornate columns I saw in Venice, I have created thick couched lines in some sections of the cloth. To make the lines as thick as possible, I've laid thick wool for the base 'threads' [**A**], then the appropriate coloured embroidery thread is stitched over the top.

To couch, bring the needle up through the fabric at one end of the base thread, just to the side. Take the needle over the base thread, parallel to the point you came out, and down into the fabric. Bring the needle up through the fabric, a little in front of the point where you first started. Repeat all the way down [**B**], holding the base thread with your non-working hand to stop it from moving around.

Finished couched examples

See how I've accented the ridged panel (left) with couched yarn on each side, extending these beyond the panel to help connect them to another block in the cloth underneath. To create a nice border for the panel, and help relate it to the variegated thread colours in the panel above, I have actually couched the border between the two in gold–coloured thread. This whole process should be a spontaneous response to the fabric patches themselves. Sometimes a couched line is used to tidy up an edge; sometimes lines separate two different fabric patterns or colours.

In another section of the cloth (below), where the panels are flatter and less textured, I've pinched and couched the fabric to create more interest and dimension.

15 Using my sketchbook work for reference, one of the smaller panels on the cloth had eight small squares placed in rows within it, with eight smaller squares applied on top of each one. The larger squares were attached with little overcast stitches. The smaller squares were embellished by embroidering four straight stitches inside to form a square, using a contrasting colour thread. Seed stitch was used to fill the area around the squares; using a cream thread was a nice contrast to the grey background.

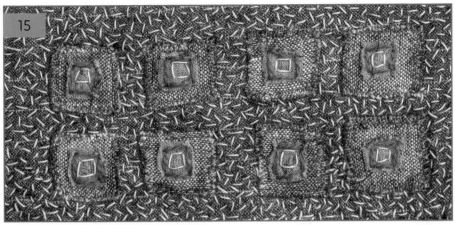

16 In another panel with smaller squares, I have used overcast stitches around the edges of the squares (as I did in step 15), but then worked simple straight stitches in rows at the centre of each square. Besides creating a different effect, this is also a lovely way of showing off your hand-dyed threads, making them more of a focal point in some sections of your cloth. To finish the panel, I then worked an outline of running stitches all around and in between the squares, again using hand-dyed thread to tie everything together.

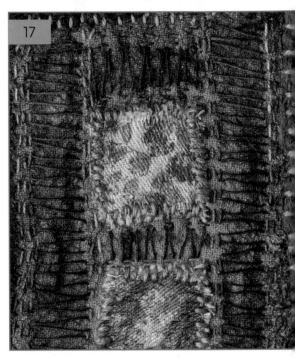

17 Small floral squares in the cloth were held down with overcast stitches, worked in a complementary thread colour. Running stitches were used to outline the squares and create small borders around them; to finish the panel, long straight stitches were used as a filling stitch.

18 As you may remember in step 4 on page 92, a layer of black chiffon was applied to dull the colours on the cloth slightly. As you can see in the photo (and in the photos for steps 16 and 17), I have snipped into the chiffon within these panels to create a little texture on the surface and ensure that little bits of colour in the fabric below can 'pop' amongst the darker areas.

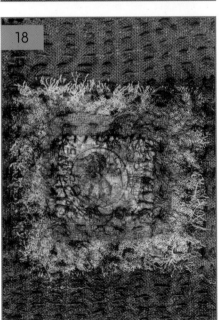

TIP

Silk thread is lovely to work with, as it just glides wonderfully through the fabric. However, it is a little more expensive to buy than other kinds of thread and yarn.

19 The appliqué is now done. In addition, decorative embroidery such as fly-stitch patterning, buttonhole wheels, couching, overcast stitching, seed stitch and any other embroidery detail can now be completed on your own cloth.

The final stage is to completely cover the surface of your cloth with 'slow stitch darning/running stitch. This stitching can, as in the landscape cloths, be worked in little blocks of stitching, with each 'block' running in different directions. These running stitches could be embroidered in straight rows across the work, but changing direction makes the surface a little more interesting.

[**A–C**] – In certain sections, I have mostly selected threads in muted colours that sit comfortably on their particular surface – we don't want to create areas that distract from the other embroideries on the cloth. But in one or two areas I have used a stronger colour of thread to pull out the colours a little more and add interest.

[**C**] – You can see here that the running stitches do not run through the area of seed stitch. This allows the seed stitch to have its own importance, and not create confusion. This applies to all areas that have decorative embroidery.

[**D**] – For appliqué patches, do not be afraid the let the darning stitch work beyond the 'borders' – the running stitches give cohesion to the cloth, and help to bring all the elements together.

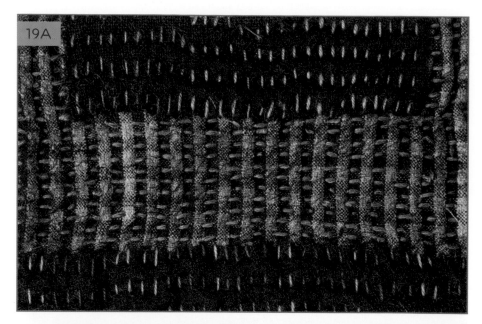

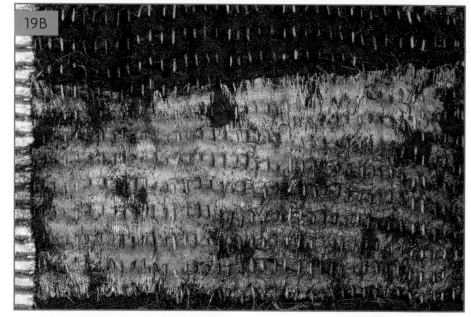

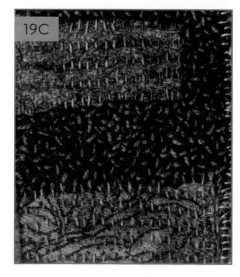

20 It is nice to add embellishments to your work if the design allows. In this instance, I have applied a small vintage cloth button. This creates a lovely focal point. There is a temptation to place a button in the centre of each square. Try to hold back; 'less is more', as the saying goes.

Finishing off

21 To finish the memory cloth, I like to make a bound edge. This could be made from a single piece of plain or patterned fabric, and this will strongly frame the cloth. I like to use short lengths of fabric that are in the main body of the cloth. The finished cloth on pages 88–89 has five fabrics that form the bound edge. Each strip of fabric is cut 2.5cm (1in) wide in varying lengths.

Cut a single strip or multiple shorter strips of fabric 2.5cm (1in) wide. Trim the outer edge of the cloth to make sure all sides are straight. Lay the first strip of fabric onto the cloth, right sides together and fabrics edge to edge. I find working from one corner is easiest. Attach the strip using a small running stitch or backstitch, 6mm (¼in) from the edges of the fabrics. Before you get to the end of the strip, finger press a small hem in the short width of the strip.

22 Lay the next strip of fabric over the hemmed edge of the previous strip, right sides together, and stitch in place as before. Towards the end of the strip, finger-press the small hem as previously, ready to put on the next strip. Repeat this process all the way round the cloth.

When you reach the corners of your cloth, trim off your strip edge to edge with the main body of the cloth. As you turn the corner with the next strip, fold flat the previous strip and start your corner at the edge of your last strip. We now have all the four sides of your cloth with strips of fabric attached; each strip is made nice and tidy by hemming that short edge of the fabric strip. The fabric can now be pressed open, with all strips lying flat and nice square corners.

We are now going to turn a narrow double hem onto the right side of the cloth. Starting in the corner, turn a hem by 6mm (¼in) then fold over again by another 6mm (¼in), and then stitch in place with slip stitch straight across one side. When you reach the next corner, simply turn the cloth and fold over the corner twice as before, this time so it runs straight across the next side – automatically, it will make a lovely, neat squared corner. You could pin this hem in place before you start the stitching. Repeat for the next three sides. Your cloth is now complete!

TIP

At this point, I should say that if you want to add a backing to the cloth it can be tacked/basted onto the back of your cloth before you add the bound edge. Personally, I prefer not to do this as I like to see the stitching on the back of my cloths. There is a narrative in the stitching that I don't want to cover up.

Venice Memory Cloth, No. 3 – Crazy Patchwork
35.5 x 35.5cm (14 x 14in)

This cloth was inspired by the 'Pawnbroker Crazy Coverlet', found in The Quilter's Guild Collection. On a visit to their headquarters it was on display, and it just blew me away, I had to go home and design a smaller cloth in a similar way, using Venice as my theme.

A wide range of fabrics were used – some vintage, some hand–dyed – including cottons and silks, and combining plain and patterned fabric. A border of rectangles surround the centre square, which is the most

detailed section of the cloth. Words that I associate with Venice were machine embroidered into two panels of the cloth. Little blue felt elements were applied, including a blue flower and tiny squares and circles, for subtle accents. Lots of decorative hand embroidery is in this piece, and stitches include darning/running stitch, herringbone stitch, feather stitch, sorbello stitch, cross stitch, detached chain stitch, overcast stitch, Cretan stitch, satin stitch, fly stitch and detached buttonhole bars. The cloth has a bound edge.

Memory Cloth – Mum
28 x 28cm (11 x 11in)

I have used linen for the base fabric; all the panels are vintage fabrics belonging to Mum. Especially for this piece, I have transferred images of buttons and a photograph of my mum onto the layers of fabric. Fabric and felt onlay appliqué flowers and their stems have been applied and secured in place with hand stitching; vintage cloth buttons have also been stitched on to echo the transferred buttons and complete the piece. A bound edge was applied for the finishing touch.

Venice Memory Cloth, No. 1
40.5 x 40.5cm (16 x 16in)

Here, I used a grey linen as the ground (base) fabric, onto which a range of vintage fabrics were cut and layered. Black chiffon was embellished over the front to defuse the bolder colours. The grid-like design was strongly influenced by my Venice sketchbook development work. Appliqué words, patches and shapes were applied initially; decorative stitches were then worked across different sections of the cloth, such as overcast stitch, couching, straight stitch and detached buttonhole bars. Running/darning stitches completed the cloth's front. The cloth was finished with a bound edge.

Venice Memory Cloth, No. 5
38 x 38cm (5 x 15in)

Another grid design taken from my Venice sketchbook development, capturing the richness of colour I so admired in many of the Venetian buildings. Again, linen was chosen as the ground fabric for the cloth. The focal point of the piece, the floral motif, is made with Indian (hemmed) appliqué, cut from silk. Other applied features are squares, using a combination of patterned, hand-dyed and felt fabrics. I used a small selection of stitches for this cloth: overcast stitch, straight stitch, couching, and running/ darning stitch. I then finished the cloth with a bound edge.

Venice Memory Cloth, No. 4
38 x 38cm (15 x 15in)

This cloth was worked in four, long, vertical sections, and was greatly influenced by the developmental work in my Venice sketchbook and Indian appliqué. A wide range of fabrics was used, from hand-dyed cotton and evenweave linen to printed and striped cottons. Once each section was made, they were attached in turn to the base fabric with strips along both long edges (except the outer edges of sections 1 and 4) to create decorative spaces between each section. Machine-embroidered words run down one of the strips of fabric at the centre of the fabric, separating the left and right sections of the cloth. A bound edge was attached all around to finish.

In the far-left section (section 1), only two details – Indian appliqué and vintage buttons – work together to create a patterned panel. Section 2, to the right of the button-patterned panel, features a panel of drawn thread work (top) and Indian appliqué flower motifs (bottom).

On the right, in section 3 there is Indian appliqué, decorated with lazy-daisy stitches and French knots, and applied shapes. Section 4 features a repeated motif – the Indian appliqué flower – at the top, and a grid design at the bottom with lots of applied squares.

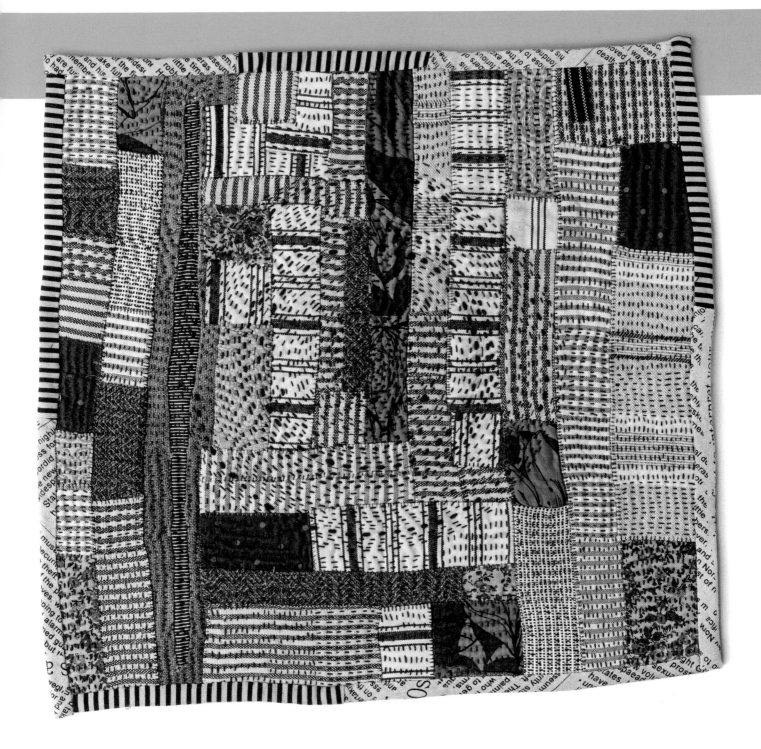

Venice Memory Cloth, No. 2
35.5 x 35.5cm (14 x 14in)

Venice is famous for its gondoliers, and the stripes used throughout this cloth are reminiscent of the gondola mooring posts and the outfits worn by the gondoliers themselves!

Linen was used as the ground fabric, then smaller pieces of different fabrics were arranged over the top to form a grid pattern representing Venetian architecture – these were mainly heavier cottons in stripes, with a few printed and plain fabrics to add interest. Solely running/darning stitch in red thread has been used, and covers almost the whole surface in a similar fashion to Kantha stitching – a great demonstration of how less is more. A bound edge was applied to finish.

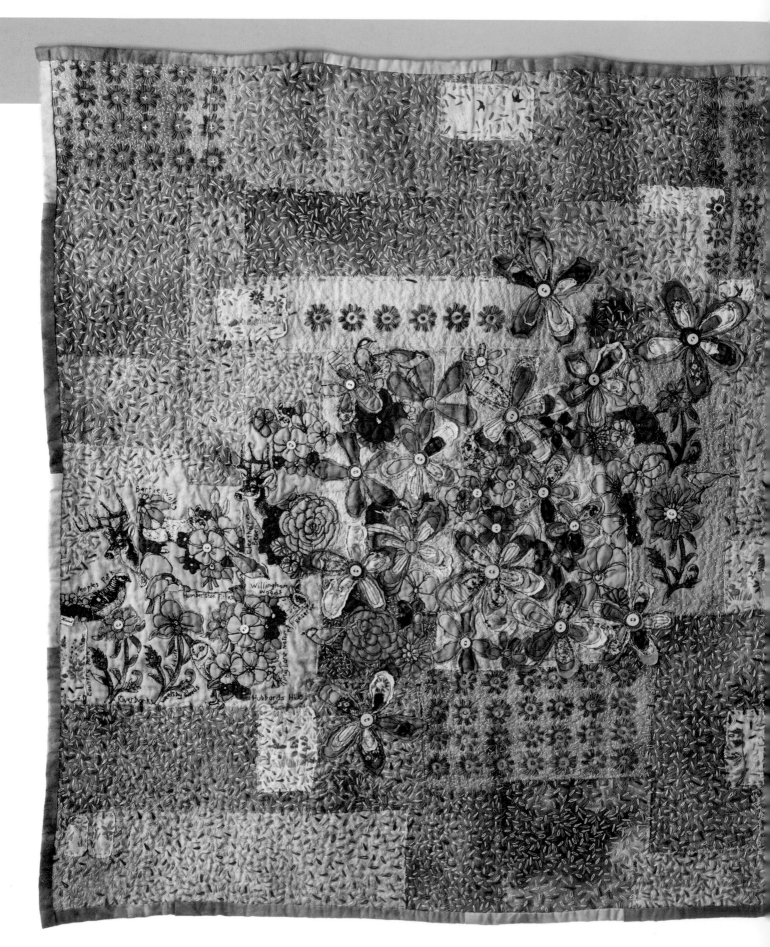

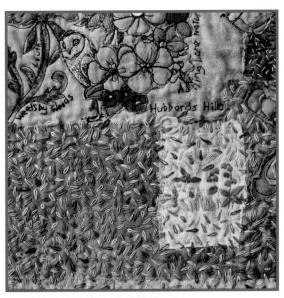

Dog Walks
99 x 99cm (39 x 39in)

This is a memory cloth inspired by the many walks my husband and I have taken in the countryside with our dog, Bertie. An old tablecloth was recycled and hand-dyed to use as the base fabric, and a selection of hand-dyed linen and cotton calico were arranged on top. Appliqué features were then included, from onlay flowers to broderie perse flora and fauna, which were then free-motion embroidered. Additional flowers have been printed onto some panels, and then decorated with hand stitching. Hand-embroidered words, describing the places where I go for my dog walks, decorate and encircle some of the appliqué in the left, central area of the cloth. The whole surface was then stitched using a combination of detached chain stitch and seed stitch. A bound edge was made using remaining hand-dyed fabrics used in the panel.

Birds, Birds, Birds

'The most satisfying thing a human being can do – and the sexiest – is to make something. Life is about relationship – to each other – and to the material world. Making something is a relationship... But the thing about craft, about the making of everyday objects that we can have around us, about the making of objects that are beautiful and/or useful, is that our everyday life is enriched.'
– Jeanette Winterson, writer, b. 1959

My studio is becoming more like the nature table I loved at school! My studio space is upstairs in the house and has a window that juts out into trees in my garden that are frequently occupied by birds – a perfect view. My lovely pair of wood pigeons, so heavy and plump, land on the branches of a beautiful forest pansy tree by my window; they, along with blue tits, little wrens, blackbirds, magpies, gulls and more, bounce the branches under their chunky weight. I like to feed them, and delight in seeing them every day in every season.

Birds have such wonderful form. There is such diversity in shape and size, and the variety of colours in their feathers is wonderful. Exploring the lifestyle of birds is fascinating. Humans seem to have always loved to feed the birds, and we as a species seem to have an emotional response to these lovely little creatures. After all, isn't it amazing to be inspired by something that is accessible to us all, just outside the windows of our homes? I thought it would be great to develop unique, fabric-and-stitch birds that one could see everyday *inside* the house!

Three-dimensional bird sculptures are perfect forms on which to develop some lovely expressive stitching by hand. The process is simpler than it seems. My birds are formed by making a paper pattern to cut out appropriately shaped fabric pieces that I then stitch together. The three-dimensional shape is stuffed firmly then finally decorated with fabrics and hand stitching. In terms of an exciting starting point for expressive textile work, our sculpture has all the design elements we need – colour, shape, texture and marks.

My birds can either appear as wall-mounted or in full form, and are then displayed on driftwood that has been collected on dog walks. Before adhering the bird to the wood, my husband very kindly and expertly cuts it and then cleans, smooths and waxes it for me.

Exploring three-dimensional forms is more of a challenge for me than the cloths. I have created bird motifs for some cloths and in many mixed-media pieces of my work, but these have been mostly two-dimensional pieces – either I make small appliqué birds that are then stitched onto panels, or simply draw or stitch bird outlines onto paper. Therefore, to make the three-dimensional approach less complicated, I take a simple approach and create abstract representations of one of my favourite animals. This also allows for slight exaggeration – the beak can be a bit stronger, the colour palette bolder or the tail a bit longer!

Birds are such inspirational, sociable and very gossipy creatures, and it seemed only right to capture them in stitch! Bird- and nature-inspired work is very current and on trend with textile artists who explore a range of techniques: from Anne Kelly and Cas Holmes to Pauline Bartnik and Mandy Pattullo, to name a few.

Developing a 3D Bird

Planning your bird sculpture requires a little more attention than a two-dimensional piece, as you not only need to think about the kind of bird you're making and the kind of hand stitching and embellishment you will apply to it, but you will also need to think about how to make the pattern for your bird, too. I have provided templates for the duck and small bird I am making in this chapter (see pages 140 and 141), which you can use if you are re-creating this design for yourself. If you are creating different birds, feel free to use these templates as a starting point for drafting your own bird pattern.

If you are creating your own bird, take some time to select it. Again, finding inspirational sources and recording them in your sketchbook will be of paramount importance – although our birds will be abstract in appearance, it's important that they still have some of the form and features of your chosen bird. To achieve this, you will need lots of sources, perhaps images of the bird from different angles, too.

If you struggle to find a good bird outline, go to the search bar on the internet and look for something like 'blackbird outline drawing'. You should find some sort of diagram or drawing that you can use as a starting point. Go to the 'Print...' icon and navigate through the window that pops up to enlarge the drawing, if necessary. Now, you can print it out and use this as your bird pattern.

You may decide to make a fantasy bird of your own design! Take features from a selection of your favourite birds, splice them together and then use coordinating fabrics and threads to make all the different body parts harmonize together to make your 3D interpretation.

The other thing to consider when making your sculpture is whether your bird will sit on a wooden perch – which means creating the bird in full, with legs, tail and all – or if you would prefer it on a wall mount, which will involve only the creation of the head and chest. I will show you how to achieve both these types of sculpture.

All my birds have been worked using exactly the same technique – applying and overlapping tiny bits of fabric to create 'feathers'. The colour and fabrics used will be determined by your chosen bird colour scheme. Hold these little feather bits of fabric down with a straight stitch in a fine machine thread, and try to use a toning colour. Once all the 'feathers' have been stitched in place, use a longer straight stitch, worked in slightly different directions, to give texture and detail to the feathers. A small padded wing can be added to each side of the bird to give a better form. I usually only apply wings to larger birds.

All decisions have now been made. Time to get on and make a bird!

YOU WILL NEED:

- **Approximately 50cm (½yd) piece of cotton calico, for the bird body:** it doesn't matter what colour it is, as the whole bird will be covered
- **Lots of fabric scraps, for the bird's 'feathers':** using the finished design on page 109, or based on your own drawings and sketchbook workings, select a variety of fabrics that reflect the colours in the bird's feathers. Always make sure you have more than necessary, as you wil be layering the little scraps over each other and a little of their overall length will be 'lost'. Fine cottons, silks and sheer fabrics are good. Do not use heavy wools and furnishing type fabrics at this stage, unless you are making a fantasy bird that needs heavy fabric
- **Machine threads, for sewing the bird body**
- **Embroidery threads in colours that match or coordinate with the fabrics for your bird feathers:** in addition to regular, solid colours, for my duck I have also used metallized threads to recreate the shiny appearance of mallard duck feathers
- **Toy stuffing/polyester fibrefill**
- **Florist's tape, for the beak and legs:** depending on the bird, I recommend black or brown shades

- **Paint brushes**
- **Acrylic paint, for the beak:** in the case of my duck, I have used yellow and orange colours
- **Acrylic varnish**
- **Beeswax and polish cloth**
- **Stuffing tools:** I like to use a stuffing fork, turning tubes and forceps
- **Wire pliers and long-nosed pliers, for legs and wings**
- **Approximately 60cm (24in) length of strong craft wire, for the legs**
- **Beads or taxidermy eyes, for the eyes**
- **Bradawl**
- **Superglue and strong craft glue**
- **Stitching tools (see page 12),** with the exception of the embellisher
- **Optional:** wadding/batting for backing the wings

NOTES:

Use a 6mm (¼in) seam allowance throughout, unless otherwise stated.

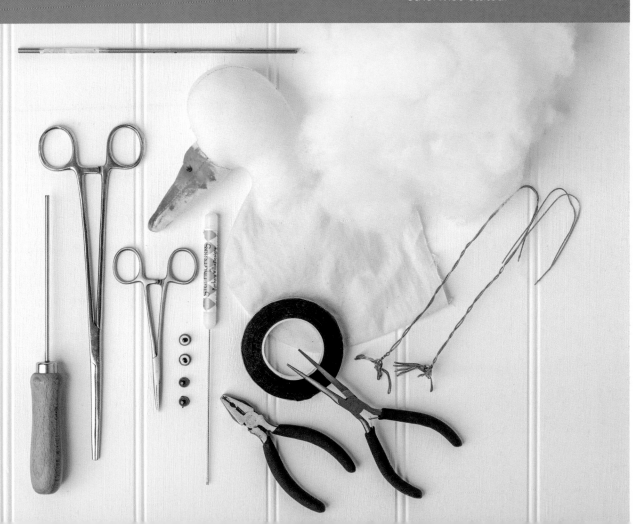

Making the bird bodies

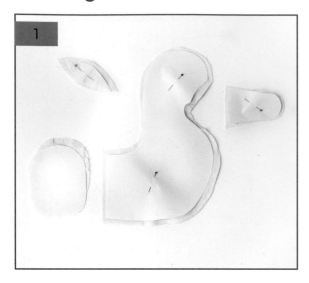

1 Make your paper patterns, either using the templates on pages 140 and 141 or by drawing up your own. Press the fabric for the body then fold it half, right sides together, to double it. All the pieces should be cut from the folded fabric, except for the head gusset, which should be cut from a single layer of fabric. Lay the pattern pieces on the fabric, matching the grain line arrows to the straight grain, then cut around the templates, adding a 6mm (¼in) allowance all around. The duck's beak is the only exception to this, as the seam allowance is included already.

2 **Duck (or wall-mounted bird):**
- Machine or hand sew the pieces for your bird body right sides together, sewing from points C to E and A to F. If you are hand stitching, use a small backstitch. Whether sewing with the machine or by hand, it is necessary to reinforce the beginning and end of your stitching with a double row of stitching; this allows the bird to be stuffed firmly later.
- There should be three openings left: one where the beak will be attached, one at the top of the head – from the top of the beak to the middle of the crown – for the head gusset, and one in the back end for stuffing.
- Once the main body pieces are sewn, snip into all curved seam allowances – this will create ease in the seam, and prevent the fabric from puckering.

Small bird (or standing bird):
- Machine or hand sew the pieces for your bird body right sides together, sewing from points E to A and F to B.
- There should be two openings left: one in the head for the head gusset, and one in the belly for the leg gusset pieces.
- As with the duck, once the main body pieces are sewn, snip into all curved seam allowances.

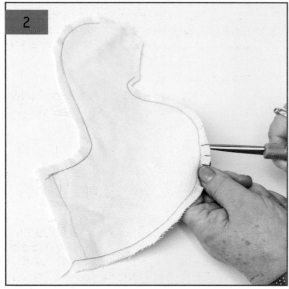

3 **Duck (or wall-mounted bird):**
- Sew the head gusset to the body, right sides together, as indicated by the markings.
- Sew the two beak pieces right sides together, adding a 6mm (¼in) seam allowance all around, leaving an opening at the straight edge.
- Pin the opening of the beak to the head at points A and B, pinning in four sections – top, bottom, and both sides of beak – and gently easing in the fabric all around. It will be advisable to also tack/baste the beak in place. The fabric may gather a little; don't worry, this will be covered by feathers.
- Machine sew the beak to the head, then remove pins or tacking/basting stitches.
- Press all the seams, including the head gusset on both sides and the beak.

Small bird (or standing bird):
- Sew the head gusset to the body, right sides together, as indicated by the markings.
- Sew the leg gusset pieces to each other, right sides together, from points A to C and D to B.
- Sew the joined leg gusset to the opening on the underside right sides together, between A and G then B and H.
- Press all the seams.

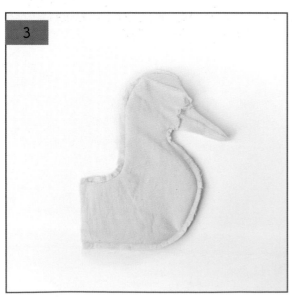

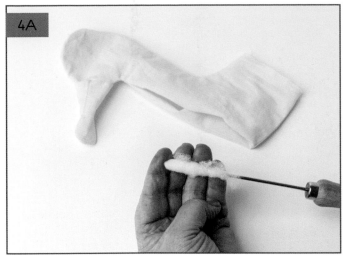

4A

4B

4 All the birds need stuffing firmly, so keep adding stuffing until the bird feels quite hard – we are not making a soft toy we are making a sculpture, so it needs to feel solid and smooth.

Duck (or wall-mounted bird) [A]:

- Turn the bird body right side out through the opening at the back, then stuff your bird with toy stuffing using stuffing tools.
- If you don't have forceps, a turning tubing or a stuffing fork, you can use the blunt end of a knitting needle or pencil to get stuffing in all the small spaces.
- Put small bits of stuffing in at a time; this will give your bird a much smoother and firmer feel. It is tempting to

make the job quicker by stuffing large amounts of stuffing in at once, but it doesn't work as effectively. You don't want a lumpy bird!

- For the beak, use the stuffing fork or pointed end of a knitting needle to twist a small amount of stuffing onto the end – this makes a dense lump of fibre and gives you more control over it.

Small bird (or standing bird) [B]:

- Follow the same process for stuffing the small bird, after turning it out through the opening in the stomach.

5 To finish sewing up the wall-mounted bird, take the back piece and snip into the seam allowance to create more ease in the fabric, as shown. Fold under the edge all the way around and pin it to the back of the bird, covering the opening. Secure it in place with hem stitch (see step 7 on page 47), leaving a small opening to tuck in a little extra stuffing, if necessary. Once happy, stitch up the opening to fully close.

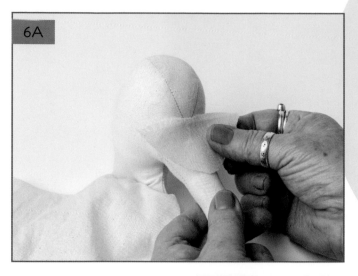

6A

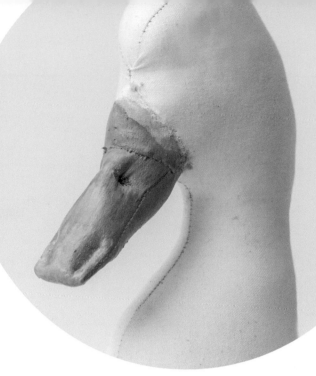

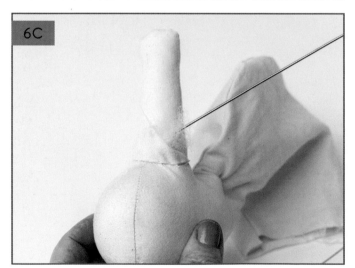

6B

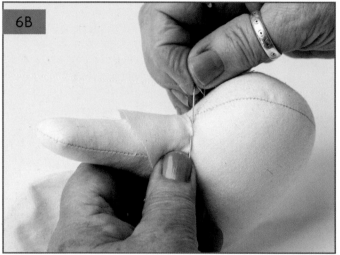

6C

Creating the beak

Large bird sculptures will need their beak to be painted, varnished and polished. Smaller bird sculptures require less work, and need just a small amount of florist's tape wrapped around the beak – this will shape up the beak ready to paint.

6 If you wish, between the join of the beak and head sections, you can create the distinctive bump on the beak of your bird. To do this, cut a roughly triangular piece of fabric as shown, then lay this over the join [**A**].

Turn under the top edge by 6mm (¼in) to hem, then secure it in place with hem stitch using matching thread [**B**].

Once this top edge is secure, hand sew the rest of the shape in place in the same way – turning under the edge and hem stitching – but leave a small gap in the bottom, rounded section for stuffing. Stuff this 'bump' slightly [**C**] – not too much, else the stitches will strain – then close the gap with hem stitch.

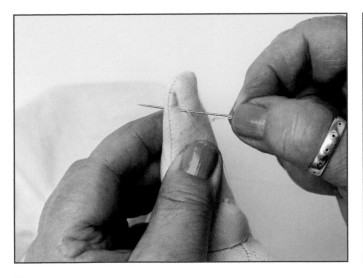

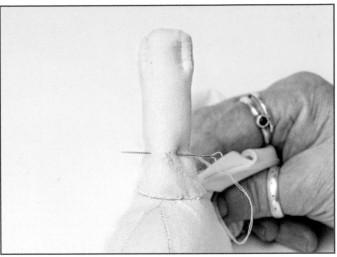

7 Many birds, including ducks, have 'sensory pits' at the ends of their beaks – two ridges right near the tip. To make these, sew lines of backstitch on each side of the beak with matching thread, taking the needle right through all the layers of fabric and stuffing.

8 To make the little air holes that birds have in their beaks, make a little stitch on one side of the beak then take the needle through to the opposite side and pull to bring in the fabric. Repeat on the other side, then make a little anchor stitch and fasten off.

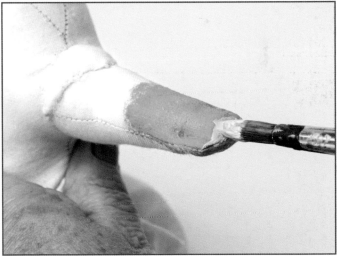

9 Rather than covering it with scraps of fabric, I like to paint the bird's beak then finish it with varnish and a polish. This makes the beak look harder and shinier, and much more realistic. Acrylic paint is perfect for this job as once it's applied to fabric, it is very difficult to remove it! Begin by painting in the top side of the beak with a medium-yellow shade.

10 While the medium-yellow is still wet, add a little pale-yellow paint to the end of the beak – this creates the effect of a highlight.

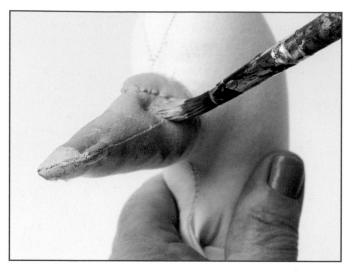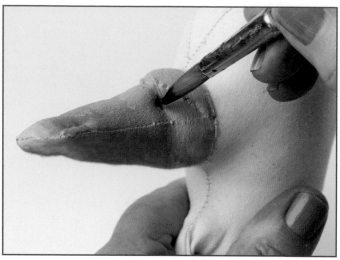

11 Continue to paint in the rest of the beak with a combination of light-yellow, medium-yellow and dark-yellow-orange, made by adding either slightly more white or a little more red to the yellow. Different tones mean different, realistic lighting effects on the beak of your bird. For example, on the bottom side of my duck's beak, you can see that I've painted it mostly with the darker shade to suggest that this area is in shadow.

12 Once the beak is painted and the paint has dried a little, use some black acrylic paint and a finer-pointed brush paint to paint in the air holes. Leave the paint to dry completely.

TIP

Several coats of paint may be needed to fully disguise the fact that your bird's beak is made of fabric. I tend to apply two coats of flat yellow first, then on the third coat combine my medium-yellow paint with the lighter and darker tones. It's important the third coat has the flat yellow combined, too, so that the paints blend better.

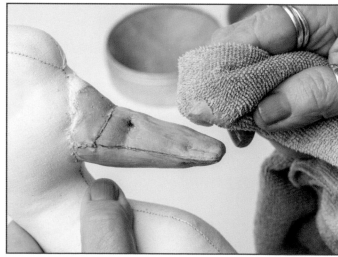

13 When the beak is totally dry, paint a coat of acrylic varnish all over to give it a little sheen. Leave to dry.

14 Finish the beak of your bird by buffing it gently with a cloth and a little wax. This polishes the beak a touch more, and adds further shine.

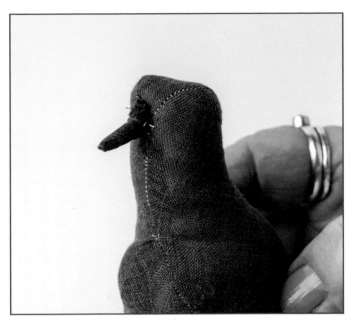

15 To create the beak for a smaller bird, follow the same process for cutting out and attaching the extra 'bump' in step 6 (see page 114), albeit on a much smaller scale. Then, using the appropriately coloured florist's tape, wrap this all around the beak. Make sure to wrap at a slightly diagonal angle, as this ensures the tape is much more secure and creates a far more credible finish. The beak can now be painted, black, brown, or yellow-orange for a male blackbird, or perhaps fuchsia pink for a fantasy bird!

TIP

The more you manipulate the florist's tape, the more pliable it becomes – this is because your hands warm the adhesive, melting it slightly and allowing more movement.

Attaching the eyes

Eyes are made with beads or taxidermy eyes. Both bird sizes have their eyes attached in the same way. Just make sure the beads or taxidermy eyes you choose are the appropriate size for the bird's head! Step 16 explains how to add bead eyes; steps 17–19 (see page 118) is the process for adding taxidermy eyes.

Before any attaching takes place, I recommend spending some time making sure the eyes are nicely lined up on either side of the head, and marking the points for the eyes with a pencil or water-soluble fabric marker pen.

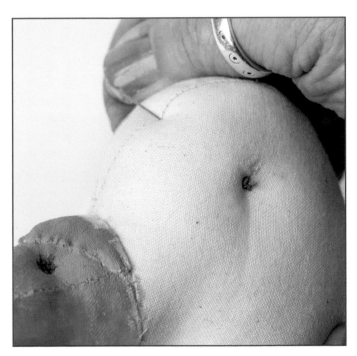

16 Before sewing on beaded eyes, I like to create eye sockets for my birds. This makes the shape of the eye area much more realistic. To do this, thread a chenille needle with matching thread (I've deliberately used a contrast thread here for demonstration purposes) and take it through the fabric of the marked eyes in a similar way to the beak's air holes (see step 8 on page 115): go back and forth through the fabric, pulling the thread each time to draw the fabric in and making a tiny anchor stitch on each side of the head to secure the pulled fabric.

To fasten off, take the needle through the top of the head then cut the thread flush against the fabric. It should shrink back inside the head.

Then, simply thread a hand-sewing needle with appropriate-coloured strong cotton thread and sew a bead into each socket, over the anchor stitches.

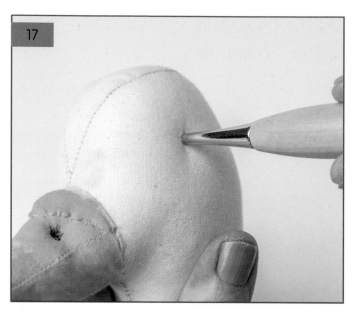

17 For taxidermy eyes, take the bradawl and puncture the marked eye points on each side of the head.

18 Trim the stalks of the taxidermy eyes to about 1.25cm (½in) in length. Squeeze a little blob of superglue into the eye holes.

19 Immediately push the stems of the taxidermy eyes into the wet glue. Hold these in place for a few minutes to make sure the glue has set a little around the stems. Leave to dry completely.

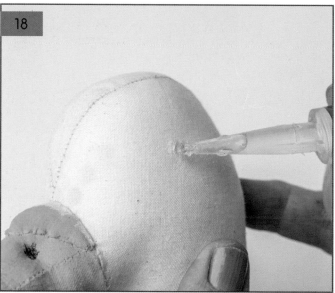

Beak and eyes complete.

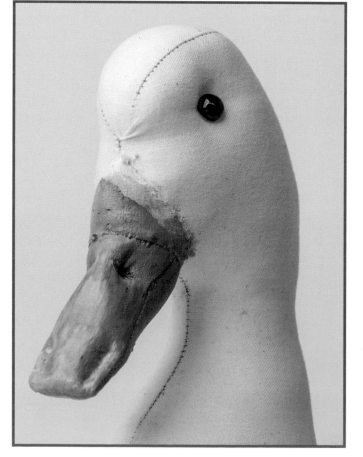

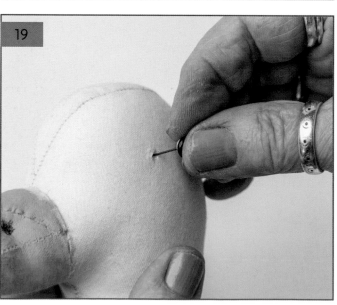

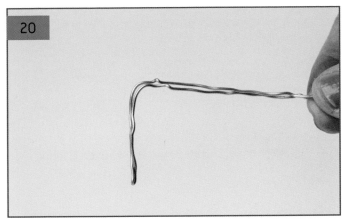

Making and attaching bird legs

For my standing birds, I like to use strong craft wire. To manipulate craft wire you will need the help of pliers. To begin, you will need to cut your length of wire into two equally sized pieces.

20 Fold one length of wire in half to double it. Bend the end over by 2.5cm (1in) or so, depending on the size of the bird. This forms the first 'toe'.

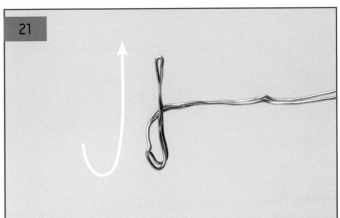

21 Twist the end upwards to make the second 'toe' of your bird's foot.

22 Use the wire pliers to squeeze the bottom 'toe' together.

23 Fold the wire leftwards, over the join between the two side toes [**A**]. Leaving 1.25cm (½in) or so of wire in the middle, twist the wire towards the right [**B**].

24 Use the wire pliers to squeeze the middle folded wire together. This will be the back toe of the foot.

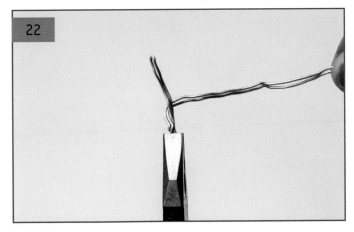

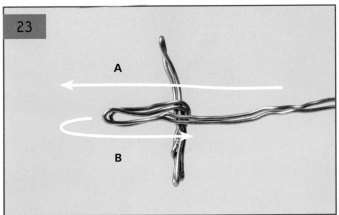

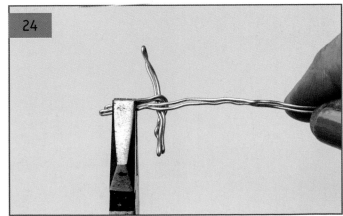

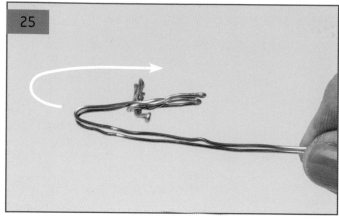

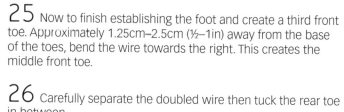

25 Now to finish establishing the foot and create a third front toe. Approximately 1.25cm–2.5cm (½–1in) away from the base of the toes, bend the wire towards the right. This creates the middle front toe.

26 Carefully separate the doubled wire then tuck the rear toe in between.

27 Start to twist the separated wire over the centre of the foot. Do this repeatedly, along the whole length of doubled wire (or leg of your bird).

28 The finished twisted leg! See how three toes have been formed at the front, and one at the back?

29 Take the florist's tape (I am using brown tape) and start to wrap it around the toes. Like the small bird beak (see step 15, page 117), wrap at a diagonal angle to cover the toes more securely and create a smoother finish.

30 Once the toes have been wrapped, continue to wrap in the same way to cover the ankle and rest of the leg.
  Repeat steps 20–30 to make the other leg.

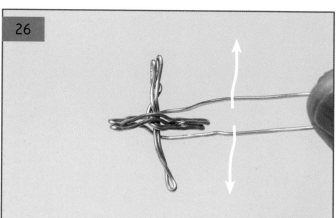

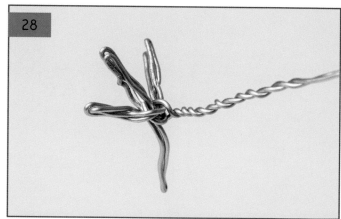

31 The standing bird body has two 'thighs' for inserting the legs. Slide a leg into each thigh, then poke them out of the opening in the stomach. Cross the tops of the legs then twist and squeeze them together – again, pliers will help with this.

32 Push more stuffing into the bird using a stuffing tool. Cover the twisted wire where the legs join with stuffing. Continue to stuff until the underside of the bird feels firm and full – this will anchor the legs in place and complete the bird's main form.

33 Secure the opening on the underside of the bird with either ladder stitch or whipstitch, making sure the opening is securely stitched. 'Feathers' will completely cover the stitches later, so it isn't a problem if some of your stitching is visible.

34 Stand your bird on a flat surface then bend the legs of your bird into an 'elbow' shape. Wrap a little florist's tape around each thigh to cover the joins between the fabric and wire legs.

Attaching feathers

The 'feathers' are made by layering little squares or rectangles of fabric over each other then stitching them in place.

I tend to work from the beak up to the top of the head, down the neck and the along the rest of the body. This follows the direction and flow of a real bird's feathers.

35 As I am making a mallard duck, I will be using a combination of green, white, orange and grey scraps in varying tones. Having your sketchbook close by with your developed design will be very useful here, to make sure you are transitioning from one colour to the next correctly.

Begin by laying one scrap in your first colour (here, the dark green) just above the beak of your bird. With a coordinating thread and sharp hand-sewing needle, bring the needle through the fabric above the beak, up through the fabric scrap. Slide a second scrap underneath (here, the light green rectangle).

36 Make a few stitches through both scrap fabrics. Try to stitch only around the middles of the scraps; this allows you to slide other scraps underneath both pieces later.

37 Slide another scrap (here, a dark green rectangle) under the second scrap and make a few stitches at the centre. Tuck another scrap (green and purple stripy square) below the first and third scraps. Again, make a few stitches in the middle to secure it to the bird's head.

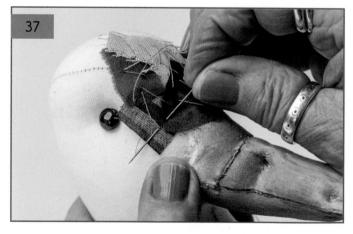

38 Continue to attach your remaining 'feathers' in the same way – sliding scraps of coordinating fabrics under the previously attached squares or rectangles then securing them to the bird with a few stitches.

As you follow the colourway detailed in your sketchbook, try to keep in mind the ways you can suggest different light sources on your bird. For example, for my mallard duck, I will use darker shades and tones of green just under the beak, slightly down the neck, to imply the beak is casting a shadow on the duck's body. I have also used paler shades around the top of my duck's head and around the beak, as sunlight would likely hit these areas of the bird more.

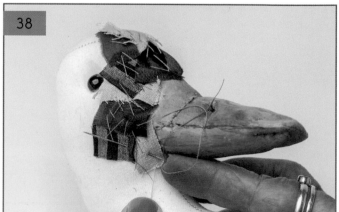

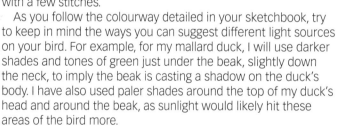
The feathers for the smaller birds are attached in the same way.

The mallard duck has a wonderful array of colours. Male mallards have a dark, iridescent-green head and bright yellow beak. The grey body is sandwiched between a brown and orange breast and black rear.

The head gave me an opportunity to raid my stash for all those lovely bits of iridescent silks and velvets. I focused the turquoise shades around the beak area, then graduated into greens for much of the head, right down to the neck. The fine machine thread used to hand stitch the 'feathers' onto the head were also in a range of green and turquoise shades. As a final layer, and to create highlights on the head, I used a lovely metallic thread.

Below the head and neck there is a white band, then the duck's wonderfully bronze breast. I used rich oranges taken from both plain and printed silks. A combination of browns blended into the orange worked very well. A variety of matching threads was used for the stitching. As you look towards the back of a real mallard, the colours become grey, pale cream and white; this is an effect I've recreated with my own duck's feathers. Lots and lots of straight stitches blend the little scraps of fabrics together, giving the unity and detail the feathers in this area need.

In retrospect, I feel the mallard needed a set of little padded wings to give it a better form. Even though I have already attached the bird to the wooden plaque, it is still possible to do this. Instructions for the wings are given overleaf, on page 124.

123

Making wings

The penultimate stage in our bird sculpture! I don't always add wings to my birds, depending on the design – and I haven't added them to my mallard duck – but they can give extra dimension to the piece. The wings are made with the same fabric used for the main bird body, backed with a little wadding/batting and then sewn onto the bird.

39 Using the back template on page 140, and elongating the bottom of the shape slightly to create a tear-drop shaped wing piece, cut out two shapes – one in the main bird fabric and one from the wadding/batting.

40 Lay the wadding/batting over the wrong side of the main fabric. Hem the edges of the wing by 1cm (⅜in) or so to round off and neaten the shape of the wing. Overlap the 'bottom' section also, to make more of a point and create a more realistic wing shape – neat stitching isn't essential here, as it'll be hidden away once the wing is attached.

41 Cover the front of the wing with little scraps of fabric in the same way as described on page 122. Once the whole wing is covered, lay it onto the bird and pin it in place. Secure the wing with hem stitch, leaving a gap in one edge. Stuff with a little stuffing then close up the gap.

42 Repeat steps 39–41 to create the wing on the other side of the bird.

41

WING ALTERNATIVE

For striking, abstract wings, you can use florist's or craft wire.

Bend three different lengths of wire – one large, one medium and one small – into teardrop shapes. Twist the ends to secure each shape.

Bind each wire wing with florist's tape, wrapping the tape at a diagonal angle to ensure it sticks securely to the wire.

Lay all three wings on top of each other; you should have concentric teardrops. Bind the wings together wherever the layered wires touch or overlap. If you wish, you can cover these bound areas with scraps of fabric, to unite the wings more with the rest of the feathers on your bird.

To attach the wings, simply lay them over the sides of the bird and work overcast stitches over the bound wire and through the body of the bird.

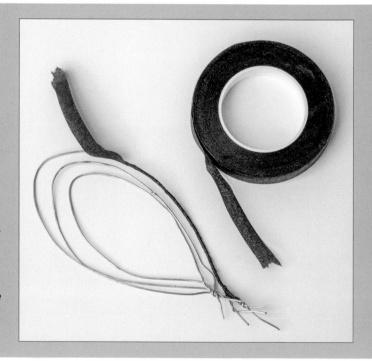

Finishing off your sculpture

43 To complete my birds, I like to adhere them to a piece of wood found in the wood or by the sea where I got the inspiration for my bird. Before any gluing takes place, the wood is cleaned, sometimes sawn and sanded smooth, then waxed and polished.

For my wall-mounted birds, I apply strong craft glue to the flat back piece of the bird then stick it to the wood. I will leave the bird to dry horizontally to ensure it's secure to the wall mount.

For my standing birds, I hammer a small staple over the middle toe on each foot to secure the bird to the wooden base. This can be seen with *Mr. Crow's New Coat*, below. With a tiny paintbrush I paint the staple brown or black, depending on the colour of the foot.

The wired wings on *Mr. Crow's New Coat*

Wired wings were perfect for my crow, as they suited his theme and motifs. I bound the wires with black florist's tape this time, and wrapped scraps of purple fabric over the joined sections of the wing to reflect the purples seen in the body of the crow, creating harmony. You'll see I have also created a bird tail with wire – to do this, I twisted three lengths of wire into tall, squashed 'X' shapes, bound each wire with back florist's tape, joined the three 'X' shapes together with the tape then stitched them to the back of the bird with overcast stitches. See also pages 134 and 135.

Small Bird

Bird approx. 13cm (5in) high, 13cm (5in) long; base 13cm (5in) high, 7.5cm (3in) in diameter

This design was inspired by the small birds that visit our garden feeders each day: blue tits, wrens, gold finches... We have so many little birds that come into the garden, and I am fortunate to have the opportunity to study them carefully whilst sat in the garden or from my studio window. They hop about, sometimes pecking food; they anchor themselves onto branches, swaying in the breeze, and they love to bathe in the bird bath. Over the last couple of years, particularly, I have had the time to sit and sketch them, which has allowed me to really understand their form and colour.

Male blackbirds I love, especially for their yellow beaks and their inquisitive pose (see page 122) – they seem such noble little birds. I love to use the combination of blacks and greys – and a mix of floral and plain fabrics – when making these small blackbirds.

Although I have studied the birds carefully, I never seem to make my birds realistic in colour. Good form is important, but colour is spontaneous. All the colours work well together in Small Bird; they are harmonious, but not an accurate representation of one particular bird.

Mr. Crow

Bird approx. 17.5cm (7in) high; wall mount 22.5cm (8in) high, 10cm (4in) in diameter

Mr. Crow was my first wall-mounted bird. He was inspired by the beach crows that follow us along the water's edge when we walk Bertie, our dog! This piece allowed me to experiment with those lovely colours I could see on the crows – purples, blacks, dark blues and greys. The beak was part of the bird body pattern, and is slightly exaggerated. I was so pleased how well it painted, and the wax and polish I gave it after the paint had dried created a perfect finish. Mr. Crow's lovely taxidermy eyes give him real character. He has two small padded wings attached to both sides of the body to finish.

Woody the Wood Pigeon

Bird approx. 25.5cm (10in) high, 30.5cm (12in) long; base 15cm (6in) high, 7.5cm (3in) in diameter

Woody was inspired by a pair of wood pigeons that feed in the garden every day. They often fly onto a tray that is attached to a tree by chains, and as they sit side by side, swinging on the tray, the branch groans under their weight – what a fabulous pair! His wire legs are bound with layers of hand-dyed embroidery threads, giving him heavier thighs and chunky feet. Long, stuffed wings were attached on each side.

Beady-Eyed Seagull
*Bird approx. 17.5cm (7in) high; wall mount 20.5cm (8in) high, 10cm (4in)
wide at the widest point*

*A piece inspired by the time we spend on the beach walking, although our local park also attracts lots
of seagulls as we are so close to the coast. For a few years, we had seagulls nesting in our chimney pots
as well. Despite their reputation, I love seagulls! For my beady eyed creation, initially I covered him in
scraps of white cotton fabric, intermingled with shades of grey torn from both printed and plain fabrics.
I also used scraps of old lace to give him a lovely texture. As for Mr. Crow (see page 128 and 129), the
beak was slightly exaggerated for effect, and lovely beady taxidermy eyes finish off the watchful gaze
for which seagulls are so famous! A piece of beach ceramic, collected from one of my beach walks, has
been pushed into the crevice of the driftwood wall mount, completing the coastal theme of my sculpture.*

Mr. Crow's New Coat

Bird approx. 23cm (9in) high, 40.5cm (16in) long; base 20.5 x 10 x 2.5cm (8 x 4 x 1in)

My beach crows continue to inspire my sculptures, but this time I have given one crow a fancy coat. First I printed some black fabric with white acrylic paint, then embellished the printing with hand embroidery. Each printed and embroidered motif was cut out and used to cover the bird. In addition to the printed pieces, black, purple and black–and–white patterned fabric scraps were incorporated. To attach the 'feathers', I used a fine black thread, secured with the typical straight stitches. Mr. Crow has an open beak – this was part of the bird body pattern. I stuffed it with the body of the bird, painted it with black acrylic paint then waxed and polished it to give the beak sheen. Again, lovely black taxidermy eyes bring life to Mr. Crow. In addition to his decorative wire wings (see pages 124 and 125 for details), I finished off Mr. Crow by sewing on a vintage metal button at the centre of one of the embroidered circles as a point of interest.

Kingfisher

Bird approx. 15.25cm (6in) high; wall mount 25.5cm (10in) high

The idea for this bird came from a dog walk a couple of years ago, when I saw a kingfisher for the first time – it had incredibly beautiful, iridescent colours in its feathers. The bird sculpture's body is made in exactly the same way as the other birds, from cotton calico that is then stitched together and stuffed. However, for the 'feathers' of my kingfisher I attached wool and silk fibres to the body with felting needles, instead of sewing on fabric scraps. The fibres were just the colours I needed. As a result, the padded wings on this bird are much more defined. Once the bird was covered in fibres, I worked straight stitches across the surface with a fine machine thread in matching colours to give the kingfisher's body a feather–like texture. The beak was part of the main bird pattern, and measures 7.5cm (3in) long. It was stuffed then painted with two shades of acrylic paint – black on the top and red on the underside. A wax and polish helps to add shine and further impressiveness to his beak, which I love! Small, black taxidermy eyes complete the focused gaze of this extraordinary bird.

137

Conclusion

This is not really the end – our creative journey continues, and it's just the beginning of a new chapter.

There are so many possibilities for new work.

Inspiration is all around us, everywhere we look. I hope this book will be a catalyst for your own creative adventure, which you can use to help you develop your ideas from your first inspiration, through the development, colour, fabric and stitch stages.

Make sure you embrace new challenges, too, as this will open your up to satisfying and rewarding experiences.

Please use the book, refer to it, but most importantly put your own stamp on any of the techniques and ideas you try. Grow in confidence in your designing, making and stitching. It doesn't matter how experienced we are or how long we have enjoyed textiles, there is always room to grow, and the possibilities are endless. I hope you will make time in your life to be expressive with stitches!

'...Embroidery is the art of enriching a fabric. [To be] "embroidered", and not just covered with thoughtless stitchery, is the result, and is one of lasting joy and satisfaction.'
– Mary Thomas, embroiderer and author, 1889–1948

Templates

All templates are 100 per cent to scale and can be traced off and transferred directly onto your fabric. With the exception of the beak piece, you will need to add a 6mm (¼in) seam allowance to all template pieces (see the dashed lines around the templates).

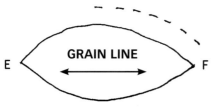

GRAIN LINE

E   F

SMALL BIRD – Head gusset

(See page 112)

Cut 1

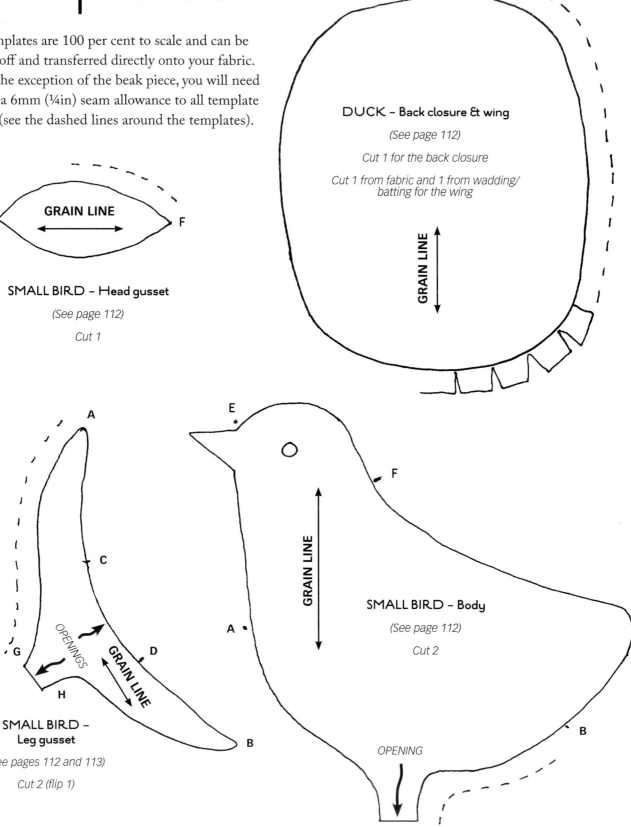

DUCK – Back closure & wing

(See page 112)

Cut 1 for the back closure

Cut 1 from fabric and 1 from wadding/ batting for the wing

GRAIN LINE

GRAIN LINE

A

C

OPENINGS

GRAIN LINE

G

H

D

B

**SMALL BIRD –
Leg gusset**

(See pages 112 and 113)

Cut 2 (flip 1)

E

F

A

B

GRAIN LINE

SMALL BIRD – Body

(See page 112)

Cut 2

OPENING

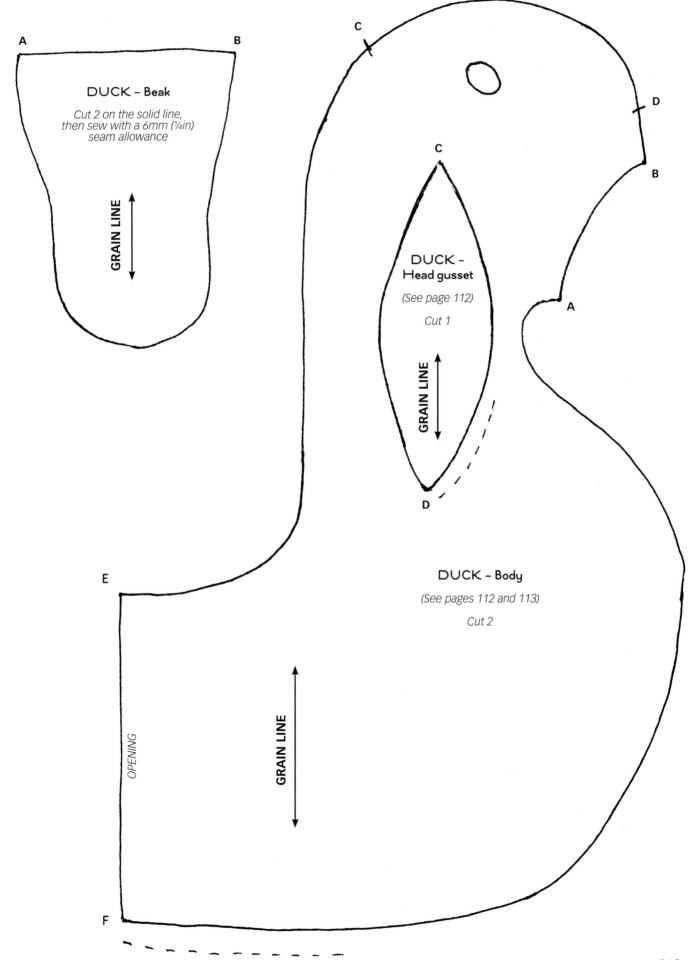

DUCK – Beak

*Cut 2 on the solid line,
then sew with a 6mm (¼in)
seam allowance*

GRAIN LINE

A · B

C

**DUCK –
Head gusset**

(See page 112)

Cut 1

GRAIN LINE

D

C · D · A · B

DUCK – Body

(See pages 112 and 113)

Cut 2

E

OPENING

GRAIN LINE

F

Index